/

MW01534099

58 William St.

Bedford, OH 44146

440-622-3507

MORNING LOVE WALK

A Book About
THE YEARNING HEART OF GOD

by

Adam Spacagna

*Discovering the heart of God through scripture,
Divine encounters, and nature.*

authorHOUSE®

AuthorHouse™
1663 Liberty Drive, Suite 200
Bloomington, IN 47403
www.authorhouse.com
Phone: 1-800-839-8640

First published by AuthorHouse 11/6/2007

ISBN: 978-1-4259-3655-6 (sc)

Printed in the United States of America
Bloomington, Indiana

This book is printed on acid-free paper.

I dedicate this book to my wife Emily
and my two wonderful children Adam and Grace.

Emily, I thank you for your love and passion for the Lord, for Adam and Grace and for myself. You have stood by us and demonstrated Godly character and unconditional love even when life gets rough. You are a beautiful woman and your love and nurturing to Adam and Grace has provided a motherly warmth that they needed and wanted so much. I pray that you will always turn to Jesus and keep faithful in your passion for Him. I hope this book gives you guidance to accomplish that. I love you and thank you for loving me.

Your Husband,
Adam

Adam, you are a smart, gifted, fun, and wonderful person, and I love every minute I get to spend with you. I am so very, very blessed that God gave you to me to be my son and I love you more then words can describe. Adam you are always so ready to smile and laugh and don't ever loose that no matter what life brings, keep that beautiful smile on your handsome face. Adam, I pray that you would always run to Jesus in all of life and for all of your life's needs. Son, no matter where you are in life please don't ever stop reading your Bible and spending time with the Lord, there is nothing more important then this! Please read this book throughout your life to help you reconnect with the Lord when you feel distant. I am so very proud of you and just think the world of you little guy. You will always posses a very special place in my heart son. I will always love you, always pray fervently for you, and when I can't be right there next to you, I will always be thinking of you.

Love,
Dad

Grace, I could have never imagined that God would produce out of me such a lovely, gorgeous, beautiful, little girl. You are an amazing person Grace and I am always in awe of you. You're intelligence, your kindness, your memorizing blue eyes, your athletic ability, your disciplined

v

responsibility, your sense of humor, on and on I could go. You are a wonderful daughter, one that fathers dream of having. My most dear thoughts of you will always be waking up with you early on a Saturday or Sunday morning and watching you pick up your Bible with that little smile on your face and sit down to read. I loved just watching you sit there and read away. Grace, my prayer for you is that you would desert the world and fall madly in love with Jesus so that the beauty you poses would not only be that of your looks, but that you would poses the hidden treasure of inner beauty that can only come from a heart that's connected with Jesus. Please read this book and create you own intimate love walk with your Lord and serve His kingdom with all your heart.

I Love You Bo Bo Bear,
Daddy.

INTRODUCTION

"He who dwells in the secret place shall abide under the shadow of the Almighty."

Psalm 91

"How precious also are Your thoughts to me, O God! How great is the sum of them! If I should count them, they would be more in number than the sand; When I awake, I am still with You."

Psalm 139:1-18

I wrote this book to unveil important Biblical truths that reveal what a personal relationship with God really is. As I searched through God's Word looking for clearity concerning this subject, the message that God illuminated clearly was that a relationship with Him is only an intimate one, and falling in love with Him has nothing to do with religion nor does it normaly take place within religious activity. The Lord showed me in His Word that true intimacy is two hearts secretly or exclusively revealing themselves to each other and creating a deep bond of love, and this is the kind of relationship He longs for. These revelations shook the very basic understanding that I had always thought was the basic foundation of our relationship with our Creator and that was experienced at church! To my amazement and growing fascination with God's heart, I discovered that an individual usually is introduced to God at a "church gathering", but does not normally fall deeply in love with Him until God Himself unveils their eyes and reveals His heart to them in secret. People have a tendency to link external religious activity with the inner affection of a person's heart. Although an individual displays an outward religious and moral passion they can still be miles away from connecting with the lovely heart of their Creator and it is only Him who can close the distance. The Pope may or may not truly be in love with God, or Billy Graham for all I know. Myself and no one else can discern weather a person truly has fallen in love with God. Only the two recipients of real "in love" passion can reveal this. Addiction to religion and religious activity itself can be a dark veil hindering a clear visual of God's heart especially when a person is highly esteemed by men, as opposed to, the non-esteemed and looked down upon prostitute of the Gospels who spilled out her most heartfelt affection upon her Lord. The wonderful thing about it is that God so passionately longs to reveal Himself to us and create a similar obsessive passion inside our hearts that draws us nearer to Him. This passion turns dry religion into a personal ocean of delight as God's heart is watered by our pursuit and fascination with Him. Then His presence begins to blossom in a daily intimate revelation of the utmost pleasure known, the pleasure of the divine character and brilliant personality that created every thing that exist. I pray that this book will help you begin the greatest journey you could ever embark upon, the journey into the yearning heart of God.

Chapter One

THE BIRTH OF DESIRE

Good morning
sweet Lord of my heart.
I call to Thee to walk with me.
I can see You this morning Beloved, walking
by Your stream, In Your garden,
Your presence has awakened the lilies,
Your lovely voice directs the songs of nature's choir,
Your gentle touch dries the dew on the roses.
You honor creation with Your entrance.
I bow with the daisies,
I surrender with the quieting of nature,
I tremble with the quaking trees.
Here I flow with my eternal love
down the eternal stream,
here I walk in the eternal garden
with the eternal King.

"The First Date"

Almost everyone has a fairly good recollection of there very first date. You can recall the preparation you went through before the date? What to wear, what you're going to do and most importantly where to go. Ambiance is always an integral factor in romance. Dinner and a movie is a good, "I need to get to know you better before I open up to you" date. The walk or the picnic basket in the park is most always a definite "I'm interested in you date". There is a greater level of affection and unveiling in the quiet and scenic moments of life then in the distractions of a loud restaurant or movie. As I began my study in Genesis, I couldn't help but wonder what was going on in God's mind and heart as He was planning His first date with humanity. As I was reading "in the beginning", I soon heard the whisper of God asking me if I could see it. "See what?" I asked Him. "My preparations". Then it hit me. The scriptures came to life and I could see that God was just like us, or we like Him. The preparation and planning, the decision to go to this beautiful, quiet, romantic garden to have His first encounter with humanity, this demonstrated His intense desire to reveal Himself to us and in essence cause us to fall in love with Him. I started to discover God's heart in an old Sunday school Bible story that I had been taught years ago. It was like a Divinely prepared romance. If there is such a thing as a perfect first date I would call it Genesis chapters 1 and 2. This sort of reminded me of the old holiday romance move "It's A Wonderful Life," where the man and woman fall deeply in love with each other in a turn of events that seemed like a divinely prepared romance. That is what Genesis 1 and 2 is, a divinely prepared romance where humanity falls in love with divinity for the first time.

"The Plan for Romance Begins"

> *" And God said, " See, I have given you every herb that yields seed which is on the face of all the earth, and every tree whose fruit yields seed; to you it shall be for food. Also, to every beast of the earth, to every bird of the air, and to everything that creeps on the earth, in which there is life, I have given every grain, herb for food, and it was so. Then God saw everything he had made, and indeed it was very good. So the evening and the morning were the sixth day."*
>
> *Genesis 1:29-31*

The first move the Lord made was to show His creation that He would provide for us all things. He wanted us to know that He is a generous God, a God that can be trusted, and a God that does not hold anything back. I believe the Garden of Eden was a place like no other place on this earth. This was a place of indescribable beauty and perfection. To put it in today's perception, Eden was like a tropical paradise, a luxurious cruise to an enchanted island to sample all the elegant foods of the earth with the most gorgeous spouse ever by your side. Complete with spa treatment and full accommodations and all the entertainment of millions of first time discoveries that you get credit for discovering. Protected by God's rule of authority, you had the option of snoozing with the inhabitants of the rainforest or falling asleep in the warm fur of a lion and always to be wakened by the soft breeze and gentle voice of your creator walking in the garden calling you for morning fellowship. The Lord had the power and resources to do anything for His creation and He chose the quiet, peaceful, romantic place called Eden to win the affection of humanities first heart. The Garden of Eden was the first place of romance and the first place of intimacy. The first thing God wanted man to experience was close affection between divinity and humanity.

> *"You will call, and I will answer You; You will long for the one You created".*
>
> *Job 14:15*

The book of Job in the Old Testament of the Bible is the oldest dated transcript of the Bible. It dates back before the Pentateuch and all other 65 books. What I find wonderful about this fact is that God reveals from the very earliest known written scripts we have about Him, that He longs for the people He created. From the very beginning of creation unto this day, God has an intense and fresh desire constantly rebirthing itself inside His heart. This desire began the first moment He saw His first created person and continues every time a new soul enters life. The birth of desire began in God's secret place of intimacy called: the Garden of Eden. I like to call it the garden of desire because that is what Eden was all about and as you get to know God more, you will discover that desire is like a flame of passion ignited within His heart every time one more soul falls in love with Him.

I believe desire was birthed in the Garden of Eden and ever since then has increased with every new soul. God created this intense feeling of desire so that there would be a pursuit of His nearness. Being that Genesis chapter two declares that we are made in God's image and likeness, we share in this overwhelming yearning to want to be intimately connected to a desirable other, an other that is without blemish or failure and one who can bedazzle our hearts and minds. This is what God had in mind when He made desire a part of humanity. He wanted us to long for His beauty and the pleasure of His nearness as much as He longs for us this way. God wanted more than reverential love, more than fear driven love, or the desire to obey out of fear for what He would do. He wants a love that matches the truest and deepest desires of His heart, and that is to want to be loved and desired just because He is Who He is, because we see His beauty and are fascinated.

Although desire takes it's strongest form with God, desire began with and continues to have competition and God ordained it this way. It was by no happenstance that Adam and Eve had an alternative choice to desire something else besides God. Obviously it had to present a strong allure in order to draw their attention away from their fascination with God. No one ever can say that the temptation the first man and woman faced was undesirable and easy to resist. For this other pleasure that is fighting for man's affection must be something very beautiful and very desirable in order to pull them away from such a magnificent Creator even for just a moment. We read in Genesis that God walked with Adam in the cool of the day. Can you imagine this, the Creator of the universe taking an intimate stroll with you through the garden. This other desire must have presented a truly strong allure to cause the man and his wife to take of it knowing that God had already instructed them not to touch it. So why did they? I have an opinion as to why but let me ask you to consider a similar question. Why do you choose to take pleasure in things you know God has isolated from His fellowship? I can assure you that it is not God's failure to be more desirable then sin, but rather it is more likely to be our failure to humble ourselves enough to be able to see a more fullness of His brilliance and beauty and then no longer chase after much less desirable things.

> *"The Lord caused a deep sleep to fall upon the man, and he slept; then He took one of his ribs and closed up the flesh at that place. The Lord God fashioned into a woman the rib which He had taken from the man, and brought her to the man. The man said, "This is now bone of my bones, and flesh of my flesh; She shall be called woman, because she was taken out of man." For this reason a man shall leave his father and mother, and be joined to his wife; and they shall become one flesh. And the man and his wife were both naked and were not ashamed."*
>
> *Genesis 2: 21-25*

In the above passage I believe God was conceptualizing what it will take to reveal His divine beauty and glory to mankind in order to create more hunger in man's heart. Genesis chapter one verse twenty-six proclaims that God said; "Let us make man in our image, according to our likeness". Throughout my years I have heard many sermons and read many commentaries illuminating what it means to be created in the image and likeness of Almighty God. What I have learned is that this single quote from God is a doorway to many compelling oracles.

The thing that applies in this study of intimacy with God is that we share not only the ability to have and create intimacy with the Lord, but we also share with God the poignancies and passions and longings that accompany intimacy. God never designed it to become a vulgar sex scene or the things we see polluting our land, He designed intimacy to be the catalyst that intertwines your heart to your lovers. God is the author and creator of pleasure. As we read in Genesis, God gave Adam to rule over all He created. It was put there for his pleasure, to fulfill man's needs. It was the serpent who lied to man and mocked God by creating false pleasure called sin. God is the author of pleasure; Satan is the author of false pleasure. God wants to reveal His heart to you so that you will fall in love with Him and be filled with the true pleasure. Satan wants nothing more than to corrupt you as to entice you away from seeing God's heart and filling you with a temporary false pleasure that will ultimately leave you very empty. He did this to Eve with the desirable forbidden fruit. From the very beginning to our present time, Satan has used perversions of pleasure to attempt to hide and distort God's character, personality, and His beautiful heart.

Our God is a God of pleasure. That's how He made us, seekers of pleasure, and therefore that's how He is. The Bible talks a great deal about His pleasure and we will get deeper into this subject latter on. One of my favorite verses about this is found in Psalm 36:8:

"They drink their fill of the abundance of Your house; And
You give them drink from the river of Your pleasure."

The pleasure God seeks after is found in you and I. The Bible says that the Lord is searching to and fro across the earth searching for those who are seeking Him. God gets immense pleasure from our love and worship of Him, He is longing for us to bring Him a pleasure that only we as humanity can give to Him. Its when a human with free will is awakened to see the beautiful heart of God that they begin to long for this true love. From the very beginning of our existence to today God has immense joy in His heart every time He thinks of you. It's at these moments in eternity that all life is given its purpose. It's the reason the flowers bloom. It's why tears form in the eyes of every man. It's the reason why trees of the spring air give such a cleansing fragrance.

Intimacy with God is why sunbeams are clothed with such rich colors that rainbows reveal. It's why oxygen and breath exist. It's why we can see beauty in anything and have emotions, yearnings, and desires that overwhelm us throughout life. An intimate relationship with God is the umbilical cord that gives fulfillment of life to humanity.

"Covenanted Intimacy"

"When the bow is in the cloud, then I will look upon it, to remember the everlasting covenant between God and every living creature of all flesh that is on the earth. And God said to Noah, "This is the sign of the covenant which I have established between me and all flesh that is on the earth."
Genesis 9:16&17

A covenant is a commitment, a proposal, and promise that can never be broken without severe consequence. God proposed to Noah never to destroy all flesh again if he would save a vestige of flesh that He could reveal Himself to. Noah obeyed the Lord's every detail, and God's plan to win humanities heart continued.

After seeing how corrupt man had become from chasing falsified pleasure created by Satan, God could have destroyed all flesh and brought everything to an end and God would have still been a just God.

As we read in Genesis nine the Lord chose to keep a remnant of living flesh alive. Why did God choose Noah? Genesis six tells us that Noah found favor in His eyes because Noah was a righteous man who walked with God. I believe Noah was an open door for God to fulfill His longing for pleasure. God was searching for a window that would allow Him to reveal His beauty to a man, and He found it in Noah. Therefore, even if it sometimes seems like God has to find a way into our lives, He simply is acting in the total perfection and decisiveness of His heart's desire. After the fall of mankind Noah was the first open door that allowed God to fulfill His yearning and longing for us to see Him.

I believe the act of God flooding the earth was more about passion and intimacy then judgement and anger. What traditional religion would teach to be only about judgment and anger, the Holy Spirit will teach you that it was also an act of passion and jealousy. Deuteronomy 4:24 says that God is a jealous God, a consuming fire. The Lord has a holy jealousy for His people and anything that stands in the way of intimacy with us He will consume. God's anger and fire is fueled by His intense passion and desire for His children. The flood was an act of passionate jealous desire to rid the Earth of the false pleasure that was blocking humanities view of the true pleasure found in the beautiful Lord.

Our God is a God of unbridled passion who longs to reveal Himself to you. He will use the circumstances in your life to guide you to His garden, His divine meeting place, where He will woo you and romance you and cause you to fall in love with Him. He wants you to see Him in all His splendor and loveliness and gaze upon His radiant beauty, so that you will comprehend His love for you. If you allow your religious comfort walls to fall and begin to see God for Who He is, the revealing process He will begin in you is immeasurable. You will begin your journey on the path of progressive revelation that will draw you nearer to God's heart. The devil does not want you to become aware of this revelation! He wants you to believe all the religious pictures of God that puts Him in a small box never to allow His full supremacy in your life. Satan wants your love for God to be impassionate, dry, or unknowledgeable. If your love for the Lord matures into passionate devotion, then God's heart's yearning is truly fulfilled. Don't let anyone keep you from seeing the beauty and loveliness of the Lord, for it is the beginning of the utmost level of pleasure ever to be offered to mankind.

Chapter Two

FROM EDEN
TO
THE ARK

Eternal Beloved
Savior, You are my hope.
I feel Your face near mine as
Your everlasting arms embrace me.
Your presence has awakened my soul.
Your love has lifted me above all my circumstances.
I rest my weary head upon the bosom of Him
Who breathed me into existence.
I grasp the gentle hand that once formed
the beautiful sunrises of our earth.
You have taken me to the uttermost throne
room of love. I have been removed,
Here I will bow, here I will worship.

"Continuing the Pursuit"

*"Now the Lord appeared to him by the oaks of Mamre,
while he was sitting at the tent door in the heat of the day.
When Abraham lifted up his eyes and looked, behold, three
men where standing opposite him; and when he saw them,
he ran from the tent door to meet them and bowed himself
to the earth."*

Genesis 18:1-2

Ever since I can remember, I was told about the awesome Christmas story, Jesus coming off His throne in heaven to be born in a lowly way, so that He may save the world. Year after year, this story is repeated throughout the world to cause people to reflect upon a glimpse of the character of God. People all over the world celebrate this historic event without really examining the part of God's personality that is revealed here. What people fail to see is that God has always had this intense desire to dwell amongst us.

Genesis eighteen is a perfect description of the desire of God to be with mankind. You will read that God comes in human form in the bodies of three men. This is the only place in the Bible where you will see God appearing in the form of three men who obviously displayed their deity as soon as you saw them. The scripture says that when Abraham saw them he ran to them and bowed to the ground in worship. This is a typical from those of the Bible who have had personal encounters with God. Remember, this is a God of intense passion who will do what it takes to win the affection and worship of humanity's heart. As you read on in Genesis eighteen, that is exactly what God accomplished. Abraham's reaction to his encounter with the Almighty is a blue print for those who desire to give God the pleasure He is longing for.

Before we get to the encounter we must understand what initiated the intimacy. Like Noah, Abraham was a righteous man with a strong desire to do God's will. He wanted to bring his God pleasure. If you expect to have intimate moments with God, you must first display a passionate desire to gratify God. Intimacy begins with sacrificial behavior. It's when you see the beauty and loveliness of another to be such a thing of precious worth that your own desires become a faded thought. God takes notice of the one who begins to do His will, to act in obedience to His Word to please Him and not just for self-advancement. Jesus made it very clear when He addressed the Pharisees with this very issue in the gospel's description. He told them that their religious acts were done to be seen by men, to receive the glory of man. God will not be robbed of His glory! You will not achieve intimacy with God, if the works you are doing are being done to be seen by men.

Abraham's response paints a good picture of how to react to an encounter with God. His first reaction was to worship prostrate on the ground, then after acknowledging that he was aware of God's holiness, Abraham did everything he could think of to please and delight his honored guest. Abraham's haste shows he was caught off guard by this visitation. If he would have known who was coming, I'm sure everything would have been prepared and ready. However, Abraham gave his guest the best he had. He had no clue how long the visitation would be or what it was for, and he still gave his all to the encounter and this is a clue for today's Christians who desire to attract God's presence into their lives and places of worship. We are trying so hard to preplan services that attract God presence and then wonder when He is going to manifest Himself. Remember, God sees what is going on inside our hearts and knows our motives. Even if a pastor or church leaders are able to convince one another that they are truly orcastrating services that welcome God's presence, God still wont be convinced unless they are open and responsive to unexpected changes He might make in their services. Changes brought about by God showing up and demanding full attention. God does not announce when He is coming. He just comes when it pleases Him, not you! He does not get into our schedule, we get into His, and this is the reason orthodoxy does not work. For years, man has tried to fit God into their lives the way man feels comfortable with. The problem is that God does not work in the realms of our comfort. He has His own comfortable place called heaven. In order for us draw God near; we have to create a habitation here in our world that emulates His in heaven, where He is being worshiped continually with immense passion. Angels and created worship beings are glorifying Him and bowing before God with whole hearts of devotion! We need to allow God through His Word to reveal to us the worship He delights in and not just follow a tradition created by a man years ago. The Bible is the path to discovering God's personality and desires. So use God's Word to create your own atmosphere of desirable worship that is very inviting to a God who already longs to be with you.

Abraham was so ecstatic about his visitation that he temporarily became a mad man running around his house giving orders disrupting whatever anyone else was doing. I can always tell a person who has just had an encounter with the Lord. They have an ecstasy about them yet without any illegal substance. People who have had a taste of God's presence, regardless of how big or small the encounter, become addicted to Him. The presence of God is the absolute peak euphoria of pleasure any human can experience. It is the most addictive power that exists.

"Eden Put Into a Box"

> *"You shall put the mercy seat on top of the Ark, and in the Ark you shall put the testimony which I will give you. **There I will meet with you**; and from above the mercy seat, from between the two cherubim which are upon the Ark of the testimony; **I will speak with you**, about all that I will give you in commandment for the sons of Israel."*
> *Exodus 25:22*

In verse eight of chapter twenty-five of Exodus, God declares a powerful statement revealing His continued desire to be with mankind when He says: "Let them construct a sanctuary for me that I may dwell among them." It is clear to me this desire of God to be with us is never-ending. Granted, the Ark is no paradise like Eden, still God is continuing His plan by doing whatever is necessary to cause man to see Him for Who He is.

One comment I have heard throughout my years in seminary was "You can not put God in a box." What they mean is that God is too greatly revealed to be put into a constricting box called religion. However, God did allow His glory to dwell in a box as long as it meant dwelling with His people. He erected the Ark and the tabernacle and tent of meeting, so that He could dwell with Israel and all nations would know the God of Israel. There will come a day when you will stand before the Lord, and when you do, you will never be able to say that God did not do enough to win your heart. Throughout the years of humanity's existence, God has humbled Himself over and over again, so that He could move in compassion and mercy. As you read the Old Testament, you will see a recurring pattern between Israel and God. A king is raised up who walks in uprightness with God, and God blesses Israel. Then the king dies, and another is raised up who does evil and builds false idols or resurrects false worship. God brings chastisement upon Israel, and then in His time, God extends His hands of mercy and compassion and restores fellowship. The Bible says that God is full of mercy and compassion and slow to anger abounding in loving-kindness. He is the One Who longs to be intimate with you and says "To obey is better than sacrifice," because obedience to Him will lead to intimacy. Sacrifices and burnt offerings just covered up Israel's past failures but obeying His voice drew them closer to His heart.

> *".... The Lord your God turned the curse into a blessing for you because the Lord your God loves you."*
>
> *Duet. 23:5*

Although Eden was temporarily lost due to our rebellion, the Lord still turned its curse into a blessing by erecting the Ark of the Covenant. Compared to the paradise of Eden, the Ark makes the relationship with Israel seem restricted and hindered due to the inhibited access given to the priest by God. Now only once per year were the priests given access to the Holy of Holies where the glory of God was manifested on the Ark. There were abstemious rules to be followed or death was the consequence. What appears like God immuring the relationship by erecting the Ark of His presence actually was symbolically intensifying it and opening future doors to intimacy with man.

Are You In Or Out?

The tabernacle that God had Moses build had three essential parts to it that reveal the depth of our love relationship with the Lord. Each of the three areas of the tabernacle held unique and specific furniture that all were symbolic manifestations of our closeness to God. The first veil you cross when entering the tabernacle leads you to the place called the outer courts. The two items here were the brazen altar and the bronze laver filled with water. This alter was where the priest would sacrifice the lambs and bulls to cover the sins of their people. Then the priest would wash the blood off himself in the laver. These acts symbolically represent a person coming to salvation in Christ and their sins being paid for on the alter by the sacrifice of the Lamb of God, and the laver represents water baptism. This is the extent of the outer courts, or symbolically speaking, the "outer court Christian" and sadly I have discovered that many live here. However, there are those who hear the voice of the Holy Spirit drawing them near to the second veil that leads to the holy place. Inside here you will find three items. The menorah, which is seven candlesticks, the showbread, and the incense alter. As a believer is led by their hunger for God into this intimate place they experience the illumination of the Spirit, which the candlesticks symbolize. As their hunger increases they begin daily feeding off the Word of God and this is the symbolism of the showbread. The alter of incense was used to release a fragrant aroma up to God that was made with aromatic spices. This represents the prayers and worship of the saints releasing a fresh and pleasing aroma for the Lord's delight. I believe that the Christians who dabble in here but don't seem to stay very long allow fear to keep them from entering past the third veil that leads to the holy of holies. Inside this most intimate place sets only one item that is the most precious and important of all. The Ark of the Covenant sets in this dark room with no windows or no man made light. The person who enters here can only see with the light of God's manifested presence glowing upon the Ark. This glorious place represents when a person has abandoned all things to experience the brilliance of the Lord. It is someone who has hungered for God more then anything else and will stop at nothing to experience His presence. So are you in or are you out? Whatever your answer is know this; God longs to bring you in. He made the way through His Son Jesus and He even revealed this with the three items placed inside the Ark.

> *"Behind the second veil there was a tabernacle which is called the Holy of Holies, having a golden altar of incense and the Ark of the Covenant covered on all sides with gold, in which were a golden jar holding the manna, and Aaron's rod which budded, and the tables of the covenant."*
>
> *Hebrews 9: 3-4*

Placed inside the Ark were three very significant items that symbolize God's plan for continued intimacy with His people who love Him. The manna for future generations, Aaron's rod, and the tablets of God's law, all carry personifications of access to God.

First is the manna. The manna was bread from heaven that would appear in the dew of each morning so that Israel would be sustained in their desert journey. In John 6:35, Jesus says, *"I am the Bread of Life, he who comes to Me will not hunger, and he who believes in Me will never thirst."* The Messiah was proclaiming that He is the true satisfaction of the hungry human soul. He is the true Manna for all who find themselves in this wilderness called life. Before Jesus came to earth it was prophesied that the Messiah would be born in a little town called Bethlehem Euphrates. We read in the Gospels that is where Jesus was born. Bethlehem in Hebrew means; "House of Bread," /beth/ meaning house and /lehem/ meaning bread. Therefore the Bread of Life for all generations was born in a town called the House of Bread, and according to the Gospels He was placed in a manger on hay in a feeding trough. As if in symbolic translation, the Father is saying, "Here is My Son, the Manna I promised, placed in the house of bread lying in a feeding trough." When a soul accepts Jesus as the Lord and Savior of their life, Jesus comes and indwells the heart. So, as the manna for future generations was placed in the Ark of the Covenant, the true Manna for all generations is placed in the Ark or temple of God's beloved Bride. Jesus longs to satisfy the hungry heart with bread that will fill the soul forever. Christ in His desire for intimacy invites you to romantically partake of this bread with Him in Revelation 3:20; *"Behold I stand at the door and knock; if anyone hears My voice and opens the door; I will come in to him and will dine with him and him with Me."*

Second, Aaron's rod that budded fruite was placed into the Ark. This rod was used as a help to Aaron and Moses and Israel throughout their journey. The Holy Spirit is the Help Mate throughout a believer's life. Psalm 23 refers to the Holy Spirit in this way; *"If I walk through the valley of the shadow of death, I will fear no evil, for Thy Rod and Staff comforts me."* Aaron's fruitful, budded rod that was placed into the Ark symbolizes the fruit producing Holy Spirit given to the church for comfort and power throughout our betrothal to Jesus. Another name for the Holy Spirit is the Paracletos, which means, to come along side of. The Holy Spirit will aid a believer in their walk with Jesus and produce His fruite in their lives.

Third, the tablets of God's written law were placed into the Ark. Deuteronomy 11:18 says, *"You shall therefore impress these words of Mine on your heart and on your soul; and you shall bind them as a sign on your hand, and they shall be as frontals on your forehead."* The book of Romans declares that faith comes by hearing and hearing by the Word of God. Nothing transforms a person's life like God's Word. In it is the power of God unto salvation. It is the only living manuscript that is impressed upon a person's heart and soul when they receive Christ as Savior. God writes His Word upon His Brides heart and soul so that she will find delight in Him. Psalm one declares, *"Blessed is the man who delights in the law of the Lord."* James refers to God's Word as being a mirror for a man to observe himself in revealing his heart. The greatest faith builder in my life is absolutely the Word of God. At the age of nineteen, I began reading the Bible on a daily basis as a source of encouragement and serenity. I was living on my own for the first time and working while putting myself through college. My Uncle Ed had told me how he would wake up every day at five in the morning to spend time with the Lord, and through his testimony I felt led to do the same. It was an encounter with God early one morning that changed my life. I got up at five and put on coffee and sat on my couch. Before reading one word, I asked the Holy Spirit to reveal Himself to me through the scriptures. I began reading in Romans and, within twenty minutes, I was weeping uncontrollably on my knees soaking in God's affection. I thanked the Lord for His visitation and promised that I would always meet with Him everyday at five in the morning. He spoke to my heart that day and said that He would always be there waiting for me. This event began my morning love walk of intimacy with the Creator that continues to this day. Through His Word, God placed me between His shoulders and embraced my soul. This is His divine loveliness and sweet affection that He freely offers to all who seek Him.

> *"Of Benjamin He said, "May the beloved of the Lord dwell in security by Him, Who shields him all the day, and he dwells between His shoulders."*
>
> *Deut. 33:12*

"Intimate Dwellings"

> *""You shall hang up the veil under the claps, and shall bring in the Ark of the testimony there within the veil; and the veil shall serve for you as a partition between the holy place and the holy of holies."*
>
> *Exodus 26: 33*

> *"Surely I will not enter my house, nor lie on my bed; I will not give sleep to my eyes or slumber to my eyelids, until I find a place for the Lord, a dwelling place for the Mighty One of Jacob. Let us go into His dwelling place; Let us worship at His footstool, Arise oh Lord, to Your resting place, You and the Ark of Your strength."*
>
> *Psalm 132: 3-5& 7-8*

True worship is ministering to God. Look at it as a date with the Lovely One who has bedazzled your heart. The arrangement God set up with Israel to enter the holy of holies in every detail has the appearance of a divine plan to romantically lure His people to an encounter of passion in an intimate dwelling. A heart that has been romanced to the point of no return and no stopping until they have reached the intimate dwelling with God wrote the psalm above. This psalm was written many years after the development of the first tabernacle. By this time in history God had revealed enough of His heart to mankind that those who sought after Him discovered the place to find Him was in passionate worship in an intimate dwelling place such as the inner chambers where God's Ark rested. Once a person gets a taste of the wondrous euphoria of an encounter with God, absolutely nothing can stop their pursuit of their next encounter. As the Psalmist wrote: *"I will not let sleep enter my eyes until I find a dwelling place for my Lord."* This is a lovesick believer passionately longing for His next intimate dwelling with the Lord. What drives a person to this intense hunger for more of God that they will deny themselves sleep or food or worldly pleasures to find the place of intimacy? Have you ever heard of a person staying up all night long praying and fasting and worshiping God all night, even if it only brings a 60 second moment in His presence?

At the beginning of my second year as pastor of a once orthodox church we began a date night with Jesus. The last Friday night of every month from 10pm to 5am, we would meet at the church and have all night worship, Bible study, and intercessory prayer. We committed for one year with a come and go as you please policy. We had a core group of 5 to 7 out of 65 that would come to all or most of these services. The first six months were confusing and challenging with a roller coaster effect of ups and downs. About half way into the year we were able to establish a pattern of affectionately touching God's heart by allowing everyone to express their own heart's love to God. I would open the service by stirring people up into worship with songs everyone knew, and usually by one or two in the morning, the Holy Spirit would begin worshiping the Father and Son through anyone open to Him. People would sing their own song to God and write passionate love letters to Jesus. Some would get lost in their own intimate dwelling in the corner of the church somewhere while others would be so exited about God that they would literally hit the streets at two and three in the morning walking through the neighborhood looking for a lost soul to share the Gospel to. Everything in our church was spiritually enhanced. We began experiencing quickened growth in spirituality and in salvations. This was a catalyst to the ministry and the church. What used to be a dead orthodox church in a crime and drug abused area became a light in the darkness. This dying church became reestablished due to hearts stirring up intimacy with God.

"Intimate Attire"

Then bring near to yourself Aaron your brother, and his sons with him, from among the sons of Israel, to minister as priest to Me--Aaron, Nadab and Abihu, Eleazar and Ithamar, Aaron's sons."You shall make holy garments for Aaron your brother, for glory and for beauty.

Exodus 28 1-2

"You are altogether beautiful, my darling, and there is no blemish in you, Come with Me from Lebanon, My Bride... You have made my heart beat faster, My Sister, My Bride, you have made my heart beat faster, with a single glance of your eyes, with a single strand of your necklace, and how beautiful is your love, My Sister, My Bride."

Song of Solomon 4: 7-8 &9-10

The Lord takes great delight in the appearance of those who come into His dwelling place. In Exodus chapter 28, God wants to dress and adorn His high priest with garments that are pleasing to His eyes and that symbolically represent His chosen people becoming holy. In this chapter, you will read how God demands skillful and exact coverings to be worn by the priest. He says in verse two: *"You shall make holy garments for Aaron your brother, for **glory and for beauty**."* It's as if God is saying; I want to dress you up and bring you into My chambers that you may experience Me and that I may delight in you. If you cannot see the romance in this, I doubt you even know what romance is. This is a God Who has created us for the purpose of intimacy. Think of every detail of everything created from flowers and plants to oxygen and molecules. All were created for God's pleasure and our romance. He is a God of great detail to achieve maximum pleasure. During the days of Aaron and the Ark, God had His priest dress according to His desire to fulfill the beauty of the holy of holies. What God did in the physical then, He does in the spiritual now. What He did externally then, He now does internally through Christ. When Jesus walked into the temple in Jerusalem nearly two thousand years ago, He quoted from the book of Isaiah chapter sixty-one saying; *"The Spirit of the Lord is upon Me."* Jesus was quoting the prophet Isaiah who was then prophesying about end time acts of God. Isaiah chapters 60-62 are prophetic words for the church of the last generation that will be raptured from this earth. I believe Jesus was quoting this specific area of Isaiah's prophecy to reveal His plan that will fulfill His promise to the church to beautify and prepare her for the marriage supper that awaits the eternal Bride of Christ as declared in the book of Revelation. This is the same God dressing and preparing His priest for entry into His inner chambers, now dressing and preparing His Bride for the moment of intimacy at the marriage supper. I have put the scriptures together that reveal God's plan to beautify the church with Christ's imparted beauty.

> *"Behold darkness will cover the earth and deep darkness the peoples; But the Lord will rise upon you and His glory will appear upon you."*
>
> *Isaiah 60: 2*

> *"To beautify the place of my sanctuary; and I shall make the place of my feet glorious."*
>
> *Isaiah 60: 13*

> *"And you will have the Lord for an everlasting light and your God for your glory"*
>
> *Isaiah 60: 19*

> *"To give them beauty for ashes, the anointing of enjoyment instead of mourning, the mantle of praise instead of a spirit of fainting. So they will be called Oakes of righteousness, the planting of the Lord that He may be glorified."*
>
> *Isaiah 61: 3*

" I will rejoice greatly in the Lord, My soul will exalt in my God; For He has clothed me with garments of salvation, He has wrapped me with a robe of righteousness, As a Bridegroom decks Himself with a garland, and as a Bride adorns herself with her jewels."

Isaiah 61: 10

For Zion's sake, (the sake of My dwelling), I will not keep silent, and for Jerusalem's sake, (the sake of My Bride), I will not keep quiet, until Her righteousness goes forth like brightness, and Her salvation like a burning torch."

Isaiah 62: 1

And you will be called by a new name, which the mouth of the Lord will designate; You will be a crown of beauty in the hand of the Lord,......... "But you shall be called "My delight is in Her", for the Lord delights in you."

Isaiah 62: 2, 3, 4

They will now go up with acceptance on My altar, and I shall glorify My glorious house"

Isaiah 60: 7

God desires to beautify you with His Son's beauty. Christ is the Altogether Lovely One full of radiant splendor and brilliant beauty, which He longs to impart to you, if you will just fall in love with Him. As the prophet Jeremiah said: *"And again will be heard in the streets of Jerusalem, the voice of the Bride and the voice of the Bridegroom."* Imagine the day when our betrothal to Christ is fulfilled, and the wedding celebration begins. As heaven's entire host is gathered to honor and rejoice at the union of the Bride and Bridegroom on the streets of the New Jerusalem, the majestic sounds of heaven's orchestra of perfected praise with an immense heavenly fragrance begin filling the air. As Christ looks into the eyes of His Bride, His heart beats faster as His eternal passion is fulfilled, and He beholds the work of His unconditional love and proclaims, "You are altogether beautiful, my darling, and there is no blemish in you. Come with Me, My Bride." Then the church in her bedazzled state, overwhelmed by His brilliant beauty and radiant glory, proclaims her vows of adoration written in Song of Solomon chapter five:

"My beloved is dazzling and ruddy," (as She sees the Awesomeness of Jesus and His glowing face.)

"He is Chief among ten thousand," (She is enamored by the beauty of Jesus and recognizes that He is the only True Beautiful One").

"His head is like finest gold." (His intelligence is unmatchable to any other).

The Bride recognizes the sweet voice and alluring presence that she knew throughout history, the voice of comfort and healing, the voice calling her into intimacy with Him. Then in unspeakable joy, the Bride proclaims to all, "This is my Beloved!" (The altogether Lovely One, as eternity continues).

Hidden within scriptures such as these in Song of Solomon are doors into deeper revelations of God, and only the hearts that earnestly seek Him are given the keys to open. They are given spiritual eyes to see in, past the traditional theology of religion and into the very yearning heart of God revealed to mankind in the divinely passionate language of the Trinity. Books such as Ruth, Esther, and Job reveal the intimate heart of the Father through hidden allegorical messages in their stories. For example, Ruth represents the Bride led by the Holy Spirit (Naomi) to get her conscience cleansed and her heart right, and go and sit at the feet of her kinsman redeemer Boaz (who represents Christ), and ask for His covering of marriage.

If you allow Him to, Christ will intimately adorn you in His beauty and splendor. If you fall in love with God, you will experience the imparted beauty of Christ to your life. This is an attribute of God's Church that will shine brighter than ever in the last generation. Allow God to open your eyes, to dress and adorn you for a moment of intimacy in His inner chambers. Just as He did in the days of Aaron the high priest, He is doing right now to all who desire to enter into the holy of holies, which God installed in humanities world to continue His dwelling with us as He did with Adam in Eden. The book of Hebrews tells us that through Christ's blood we can boldly come to God's throne. As the high priest had to put on his priestly garments to enter into the inner chambers where God's glory and presence was, we put on Christ who dresses us in His righteous garments of splendor so we too can experience the Lords manifested presence.

Prior to the fall of mankind, intimacy with God was conceived with an uninhibited, freedom. The boundaries of God's Garden of were few, and the freedom revitalized the spirit of man. God promises the ecstasy of this divine meeting place to us during the millennial reign of Christ, and the Church will one day again experience Eden's uninhibited intimacy. Although no man knows exactly when that will be, we can now implement the means into our garden of intimacy with God while we wait for Him to restore Eden to mankind. As you read in this chapter after the fall of man, God moved Eden into the Ark in order to continue His plan.

We learned that through the Ark and all its fullness God improvised for man, so that we could still experience intimacy with Him while we wait for Eden to return. What He did with the Ark worked for all generations before and after Jesus' first coming. I hope you are beginning to see the beauty and loveliness of the Lord and how He desires and longs to dwell with you and reveal Himself to you. I believe for years the devil has worked to block the minds of humans, so that they don't see the true image of God. I believe most people don't see the true character and personality and loveliness of God but have a very limited knowledge of Who God really is, and this is what hinders the much-desired intimacy He longs to have with them. The world needs a new paradigm of God. The Bible is a window into God's beautiful heart that will lead you to finding your own secret place with the Creator. Allow God every morning to put His garden of intimacy into the Ark of your heart by the Spirit revealing the Beautiful Savior.

Chapter Three

GROWING IN YOUR LOVE

Sweet Lover of my Soul,
Remove the thought of having to
live without You.
Awaken my senses to behold
Your presence, oh Gentle Shepherd,
Keeper of eternity.
Lift me out of the mire of this day.
Transform my carnality
with grander glimpses of the heavens.
Expand my finite sight with
eagle's eyes that soar over the eternal
mountains and sweep through
the eternal valleys of lilies where the
Sweet Son of God is awaiting
my visit. Call for me again Lover,
Capture my heart this day.

"Maturing in Love"

"Behold, I stand at the door and knock; if anyone hears My voice and opens the door, I will come in to him and will dine with him, and he with Me."

Revelation 3: 20

Before we learn how to hear God's voice, we have to discover how He hears ours, not the sounds protruding from our lips, but the voice of our hearts. This is voice that reaches the inner depths of God. This is the voice that awakens intimacy and stirs up the passion of the Godhead. The voice of humanity's heart crying out for the true pleasure found in the only true God. You will begin to hear the voice of God's heart when He begins to notice the voice of yours. God says in His Word: *"Acknowledge Me in all your ways and I will give you the desires of your heart."* When we discover the knowledge of God's character and the beauty of His personality, our hearts begin to bond with Him. God is saying that by us coming to the intimate knowledge of Him, He will satisfy the only true longing in our hearts. He knows the true desire of humanity's heart is the pleasure of His presence found in intimate moments with Him. God will fulfill this longing, if you would simply get to know Him for Who He really is?

You might be thinking; "Isn't that what church is for? Getting to know God." Church is for assembling together with other believers for corporate fellowship and worship. You may become aware of God at church, but you do not truly get to know God at church. Falling deeply in love with another person does not happen on group dates or high school reunions. You can't truly get to know a person when they are around other people, for it is in the company of many that we all tend to put on our personage. Even in the presence of only your lover, you can tend to hide your true self. Love grows strong in intimate moments, and it's in the intimate moments of life that love is matured. Our love for God begins to mature when we begin to seek Him outside of church, when we commit to spending alone time with Him.

At wedding celebrations, family and friends view two well-dressed, beautiful people in love and putting on their best image. The bride and groom appear so happy and everyone witnesses the act of two becoming one. Although legally speaking the two newlyweds are married, physically and spiritually they have not become one flesh. Intimacy has remained at a publicly acceptable level until the wedding night. It will not be until the wedding night, that in secret, true intimacy occurs as the bride and groom will begin to reveal themselves to each other. This is where the conception of love begins and matures. It is in the secret place that the unveiling begins and sacrifice, trust, passion and beauty are revealed. It is the same with God. He who sees you in secret, meaning that He sees you as no one else can, reveals Himself in secret. The secret place is where intimacy with God takes its strongest form and causes love to grow and mature. Hebrews four twelve tells us that the Word of God is a discerner of the thoughts and intents of the heart. God's Word revealed in public brings people to repentance and acceptance, but God's Word revealed in secret brings the soul to a place of hunger, thirst, and passion.

> *"But you, when you pray, go into your inner room, close*
> *the door and pray to your Father in secret, and your Father*
> *Who sees what is done in secret will reward you."*
> *Matthew 6: 6*

Jesus spoke these enticing words to the heart that longs for more than religious rewards given by men. The Bridegroom is calling the bride into His inner chambers where the revelation of the beauty of God is the reward. It is in the secret place that you experience the divine loveliness of God, and your love is matured past those who remain in the outer courts. Immature love is happy with the reward of the outer court for it is a place of acceptance that allows people to experience God in their own comfortable way.

As I said earlier, the tabernacle of the Old Testament had three areas to it: the outer court, inner court, and holy of holies. These three areas spiritually represent the depth of our relationship to the Lord. All three levels have specific furniture that holds unique symbolic manifestations of humanities journey into the throne room of God. The Lord revealed His throne and tabernacle in heaven to Moses who created a human version of it on earth. God did this, so that His presence could dwell with His people and to map out the plan for the Messianic temple to come. These three levels need to be regularly studied so that you consistently understand where you are in the journey and how to go deeper. Let's look at more revelation about this amazing tabernacle and its purpose in our relationship with the Lord.

"The Three fold Unveiling"

The first veil you cross in your journey into God's inner chambers is the pathway into the outer courts that I like to describe as the place of our courting in immature love. Since the fall of man in the Garden of Eden, our relationship with the Lord must begin here in the outer court. No longer can it begin in wholeness and pureness as it did with Adam. We now must embark on a hunt for God's closest intimate garden. The courting begins in immature love, and because of the immature stage of our love for God, the devil's attacks are most effective here in stopping Christians from growing in their love. After a person commits their life to Christ, they face many more important decisions in their journey that determine the resonance of intimacy with their new Savior. As important as trusting in Christ's sacrifice of Himself for your sins, it is equally as important to trust Him to draw you to the place of mature love found in intimacy with Him. For example, what would be the point of a man and woman getting married without ever consummating their relationship? Picture it: a huge wedding celebration is prepared, and all the guest come to celebrate the union of two becoming one then all the rejoicing and feasting and dancing takes place. Everyone gives the two newlyweds their blessings, and after it's all over, the two go back home to their own parents' houses and live separately the rest of their lives never coming to intimacy with each other. I sadly tell you that I believe this is the way many people have chosen to live their Christian life.

Jesus tells of a similar story in a parable He spoke of found in Matthew 22. Jesus describes a king who prepares a wedding celebration for his son. This king first sends invitations out, and the chosen would not come to the wedding. He then has those who would not come destroyed and sends out invitations to the highways to all who would come to the wedding feast not just his chosen but both good and evil. Verse 11 adds an astounding revelation to the story. After the wedding hall is full, the king comes to look at his guests, and in doing so he notices a man not wearing wedding garments. He asked the man as if he was shocked, "How did you come in here without wedding garments?" Understandingly the man stood speechless, and the king had him bound up and cast into the outer darkness where there is weeping and gnashing of teeth. Only the man without wedding garments on was ejected from the wedding. As you read in chapter two, God's priest who entered into the holy of holies to minister to God had to wear specific garments. The book of Hebrews calls Christians God's priests who have a boldness to enter into the holy of holies. As I also said in chapter two, this is done as we allow Christ to dress and adorn us in His beautiful garments, for it is through Him, the High Priest, that we can enter the holy of holies. Therefore, I find it interesting that the king, who represents God the Father, had the man who had no wedding garments on for the Son cast into the outer darkness. This parable leads me to seriously examine my heart. Am I allowing Christ to dress me in His garments by worshiping Him and seeking Him daily? Do I desire more of God, or have I become satisfied with where I am? According to that parable, the most important thing to achieve is preparation for the coming wedding feast.

Remember, the outer court is the beginning of our relationship with the Lord. This is the place symbolizing our public acceptance of the perfect sacrifice and then cleansing by water baptism. The two items in the outer courts were the bronze altar and the laver filed with water. The altar was where the sacrifice of the lambs and bulls took place, and the laver was where the priest washed himself after the sacrifice. These two items are only a part of man's tabernacle on earth and not God's tabernacle in heaven, for in heaven there is no need to sacrifice for sin.

After salvation and baptism, too many people stop at this point and do not seek the rest of the journey. The outer court, (also known as the place for the gentiles), is commonly found in most churches today. I believe the trend of seeker friendly churches fit this description of the outer court relationship with the Lord. They plan a service of human entertainment and media enhanced messages to fascinate their attendees so that they will come back to their church. Seeker sensitive churches primary strategy is to never offend or to make uncomfortable. This type of comfortable evangelism would work, if salvation did not require a life changing circumcision of the heart. Without getting into a theological debate over this theory of evangelism, I would like to touch upon the heart of the matter. I have attended many churches that have embraced the seeker friendly and seeker sensitive strategy. In all of them I have discovered similar corruption when the church leaders take their congregation in this direction. The first thing I clearly noticed was a hazardous change in focus. No longer are these churches working hard to grow their congregation spiritually, but is now primarily seeking to just grow the congregation numerically. Campaigns of spiritual growth and devotion to the Lord are replaced with programs that are designed to attract people to the church because of a popular named book or attractive and appealing forms of entertainment with always a non-offensive environment and this is a contradiction to the Gospel. Remember when Jesus said" blessed is he who does not take offence at me." He must have been assuming that the gospel would be a hard pill to swallow for many. It's imposible to avoid offending the carnal nature in all humans and present the true Gospel message. To say it simply, you don't change the pure truth, just to coax a person into faith in Christ just so you can have a financially thriving church, however you can do everything you can to try to reveal God's beautiful heart in scripture and pray that they fall in love with Him the way He intended. Study the way Jesus presented the true Gospel and see if He embraced the seeker friendly approach to changing lives. I wonder if He used non-offensive words and stories.

If all anyone had to do to experience intimacy with God was to attend church and believe in Jesus, then seeker friendly churches would be the key to revival. Although this system sounds easy and acceptable to most religions, the journey into God's intimate chambers has nothing to do with easiness and comfort. A perfect example is given to us in 1st Chronicles 15 where you will read what it took David to get the Ark representing the manifest presence of God into Jerusalem. There was nothing neither easy nor comfortable about this task. The first thing to bring attention to is the intense passion David had to own that would drive him to succeed at getting the Ark into Jerusalem. Therefore, keep this in mind as you begin to discover the physical travail of such a process as bringing the Creator of the universe into the realm of your cognizance. David had to follow God's specific instructions pertaining to moving the Ark from Obed-edom's house to Jerusalem, such as the priest sacrificing rams along the way of this estimated ten mile hike. Just consider carrying this heavy Ark for ten miles, after every so many specific steps having to stop and set down the Ark, slaughtering, preparing and offering a huge 1,000 lb. animal. This was no comfortable, non-offensive friendly environment but the reward of God's manifest presence was so worth it! Just imagine the odor! Yet, when the Ark did finally arrive at Jerusalem's gates, David danced himself silly overwhelmed with unspeakable joy, because a thousand years of physical comfort can't compare to just moments in the presence of God. As David himself wrote, "Better is one day in God's house than a thousand elsewhere".

Immature love stays comfortable unless pushed or drawn deeper into maturity by removing comfort barriers or reveling greater pleasures. Too many churches are failing to do this because of the "F" word. Fear! They are too afraid of offending their faithful tithes or afraid of making people uncomfortable with passionate worship. Anything done outside of faith is sin and when you allow fear of man to control you, you have missed faith. Maturing in your love for God is embracing His moves in faith. Embracing God's moves regardless of the rejections of others is an act of spiritual maturity, and I believe this kind of faith and devotion touches God's heart. Immature love is too concerned about protecting friendships, staying within comforts and not appearing too passionate about the Lord. Mature lovers are more concerned about their spouses than themselves. Mature Christians are more driven to protect God's image by obedience than their own image by attracting attention to themselves.

Every Christian has to become knowledgeable about immature love; for it is here that the enemy is most successful. If you are puffed up into believing you have it all together concerning your walk with Christ, then you would lack the humility and motivation needed to mature past the second veil called the Holy Place and eventually into the Holy of Holies where the enemy cannot reach you. Don't let the devil convince you that you are something when you are not therefore deceiving yourself, but rather proudly admit that your love for God is immature but genuine! Just because your love is immature does not mean that it is not genuine. This is what the enemy wants you to believe when you stumble, that your love for God is not real, that you're a phony, but you are not! You are a genuine lover of God, if Christ planted His seed of love in your heart, and the Spirit will water it if you let Him.

"The Taste of Unripe Fruit"

As I look back at my beginnings in ministry work, I think of words like presumptuous and premature. I think of all the damage that is caused by soldiers put into leadership positions without completing boot camp and the chaos that follows this bad move. Leaders who are walking in immature love lead people in spiritual circles instead of up the spiritual mountain. This type of leader may experience a great deal of success in their ministry and be known by other immature Christians as mature, but their success comes from their spiritual gifts and not there spiritual maturity. They are driven by a different kind of love than a true lover of God: a love for power, ministry, spiritual gifts, and achievement, **a love for the calling but not for the Caller**. A true lover of God is driven by their love for their God. These are led by the voice of the Caller leading them into intimate fellowship and not the voice of the calling leading people into Christian circles.

Unripe fruit leaves a bitter taste in your mouth that can take a long time to get rid of. Although I didn't know it, when I took my first pastorate position at age 25 I was unripe fruit. At this time in my life, I felt very driven and determined and gifted in nearly all areas of ministry. I felt I could preach convincing and inspiring messages and lead people in worship, but because of my immature love for God, I could not set the Godly example that the church needed to be able to receive instruction from their pastor. Many times I allowed my emotions to overshadow the needed discernment for problems that arise. I allowed my mouth to be loosed and would allow silly and foolish talk often in front of church attendees. Because I was not seeking God passionately and truly desiring to discover His ways, I struggled to be an effective leader. Initially the first two years of the ministry seemed to be great and successful. We saw God work in very miraculous ways even though I was hiding that fact that I had a failing marriage and was depressed most of the time. By the third year, the bitter taste of my fruit set in, and in great pain I resigned as pastor and went through a painful divorce and custody battle for my two children. Although I hurt many people and felt like a huge spiritual failure, God still desired to reveal Himself to me. He never left my side during the most painful time of my life and He helped me get residential custody of my children and a fresh start on life. Over the next few years, God had to get me to the place where only He mattered, and only His love would be the center of my passion. I had too much pride that hindered my relationship with the Lord so He allowed the devil to use many people to slander me and break me down. This caused me to seek His presence all the more.

Sometimes God has to strip things away to cause us to focus on the true substance of life, for it is through knowing pain that we see Him. Many of us are too afraid of pain and spend most of life trying to avoid it, and its not until we embrace it that we discover that pain is an open door into a deeper reality of God. The prophet Isaiah's famous messianic description tells us that the Christ is acquainted with grief, a man of sorrows. People make acquaintances all the time whether at church or work or in their local town. However, I rarely see people deliberately acquaint themselves with grief or pain or sorrow but rather take every step necessary to avoid such things. During my years of Christian fellowship, I have been in many different churches, and in nearly every church I have attended, I have always noticed a reoccurring disappointment. There is always at least one person in the church that suffers from something that makes them unpopular. It could be they are weird in some way or smell bad or their appearance is unpopular due to obesity or blemish or maybe they just have a difficult personality. Whatever the issue, no matter what church I attend, I never lack to see people as excited to see these types of saints as they are to see the pastor or worship leaders or singers or whoever fills the roles of church popularity. They run to greet so and so and hurry to hug him or her, but rarely do I see a person hurry in to fellowship and love the unpopular ones of our churches, and these are the saints I believe our Lord would acquaint Himself with first, if He decided to visit your church.

Understanding immaturity brings you to a place of revelation and change. Revelation always leads to some kind of change either good or bad, but it does not allow you to remain unaware and therefore unchanged. Our journey into intimacy with God is just that, a journey, not an overnight occurrence. You need to study the Word of God to discover the light of the path into God's chambers and simply obey out of love for Him. As I said, this journey begins when you accept Christ's sacrifice for your sins and then allow the Lord to romance you into the secret place of intimacy where love is matured. So far in this chapter we have examined some appearances of immature and mature love, now lets look at those caught in-between.

"I arose to open to my Beloved; and my hands dripped with myrrh, and my fingers with liquid myrrh, on the handles of the bolt. I opened to my Beloved, but my Beloved had turned away and had gone! My heart went out to Him as He spoke. I searched for Him but I did not find Him."
Song of Solomon 5:5-6

"Lovers Seeking Maturity"

This passage from Song of Solomon describes the close encounter of a lover seeking maturity. This lover was in the right place doing the right thing in order to get this close to the next encounter. The Beloved was at the door ready to open and come in and something turned Him away! As the lover recognized the Beloved was at the door, you will read how she hesitated, then arose from the bed and ran to the door then opened only to find a trace of the visitation. Her hands dripped with the fragrance of His presence, but He had turned away and left. We see the agonizing cry of the lover's heart as she listens to His voice calling her. She searches for Him more, but does not find Him. What drives her so passionately? How did she get Him so close, and why did He turn away? These are questions that I desired to have answered when I discovered this passage, for in it reveals an example of a God moment brought to an agonizing end. Has this happened to you? Have you felt so close to God, overcome by His presence, maybe even smelling His fragrance, and the very next moment, nothingness overcomes your senses? How does it leave you feeling? Do you feel frustrated? Or does hunger for more fill your spirit? Maybe that's why the Beloved turns away, to create more hunger in a hungering heart. Whatever the answer is, this story should have a familiar ring to those who are seeking a more mature love relationship with the Lord.

As I read this passage, I notice all the familiar ingredients of the recipe to this story. The lover is in the place where love is matured. She has gone to her bed, maybe symbolizing her "prayer closet", to spend time with the greatest love of her life. As she travails on her bed of anticipation, she finds her way through the darkness of a finite mind searching for a crack of light to peek through that she may direct her soul toward praying ever so carefully not to talk over the potential sound of her Beloved's voice. As her hope fluctuates, all she holds onto is the last encounter she had. Knowing there is more, she begins to call out His name. Within a second, the spiritual light or awareness she had opens to a radiant beam of divine glory, and her human senses become exceedingly refreshed. His voice, His scent, His nearness all becomes a reality. Nothing else seems to matter. No other thoughts exist in her mind. There's just light, peace, stillness and serenity. Before she could sing a song, say a prayer, or alter her posture, there is a knocking, a frightening yet inviting reality gently seeking her fascinated awareness--almost like a beautiful pearl doorway into a fanciful garden more peaceful and elegant than humanly possible--a soft glow of warm light covering an earth as transparent as refined gold yet as soft as silk to the touch--vegetation and life as mysterious as unknown galaxies yet as gentle as a falling leaf--so inviting, yet all guarded by a mystifying presence. Forgetting her safety is within her Beloved's care, she hesitates and looks back to what she already experienced--what she already finds comfort in. As the reality of her encounter reverses, she gives a human attempt to reach for the pearl door only to be left with the fleeing beautiful aroma and fading gentle voice of her Beloved.

You need to rely on God's power, God's desire, God's will, and not your own ability to reach more mature encounters with Him. Maturing in love has a great deal to do with yielding, trusting, and accepting, and little to do with trying and controlling. God passionately longs to have intimate experiences with you, and He is intervening in your life to bring you to the place of hunger.

Revelation always leads to change and change is better than no change. The people I am concerned for are those that are in no way affected by God's revelations of Himself. The Holy Spirit seems to work more effectively in the midst of change whether you think it's good or bad. God does not seem to respond well to the unchanged. As Christ spoke to the church of Laodicea in the book of Revelation, it would be better for them to be either hot or cold than to remain lukewarm. Even salvation comes through change. Once you accept the gift of Christ's death and resurrection, then the Holy Spirit comes and makes His home inside you and begins to change you. Maturing in love is usually not an instantaneous process but rather a slow one with many mountains and valleys. As you begin to be revealed of God in deeper ways, do your best to examine yourself without allowing the devil to plant seeds of condemnation and guilt in you. Remember just because your love may be weak and immature does not mean it is hypocritical. If Christ has planted His seed of love in your heart, your heart is eternally occupied by a power that is above all powers that exist. Simply begin to yield to the Holy Spirit and allow Him to water the seed and cause it to grow beyond fear and sacrifice and into passion and obedience. Remember the One who completed the galaxies, framed the earth, ignited the burning of the sun, is the One who completes you, frames your world, and ignites your burning heart for Him.

Chapter Four

THE ALURE OF GOD

I desire to inherit the wind,
Eternal breeze seduce my spirit,
influence my will so I don't astray.
Arouse my love; I'm ready to go with You.
Sweet wind come, I'm standing
at the edge of Thy mountain; Blow!
Delight me. Allure me Fair One,
I'm ready to fly with You.
You have me so close to capturing
eternity present, the eternity
placed in my heart. I yearn this day
Lord, have Thy own way. I wait
for You Beloved, I wait
to inherit the wind today.

"The Place Of Acceptance"

"Therefore, behold, I will allure her, bring her into the wilderness and speak kindly to her. There I will give her vineyards from there, and the valley of Achor as a door of hope. And she will sing there as in the days of her youth, as in the day when she came up from the land of Egypt. It will come about in that day, declares the Lord, That you will call Me Husband and will no longer call me master. "

Hosea 2:14-16

In moments prior to a proposal of marriage there tends to be a great amount of mystery, wonder, nerves, and excitement because the next moment after this question is asked brings an acceptance or rejection. The courtship leading up to this monumental moment between a man and woman coincides with the allure of God. In the Old Testament, Israel was referred to as God's wife and in the New Testament; the church is called the Bride of Christ, so God has always passionately searched for individuals who would become His chosen bride. With a prodigious heart He allures them away from all their other lovers where He asks for a commitment of unconditional eternal love to Him. The wonder, nerves, excitement, and the acceptance or rejection all are a part of God's design to win your heart. This place He allures you to is the place of acceptance, the place where the river of God runs right through the garden of God. The place of acceptance is right at the rivers edge where the one who commits to entering can never turn back. For this river takes you on a journey into eternal pleasures and profound divine revelations that is unrecoverable to the human spirit. In this chapter I want you to identify in your own life God's alluring presence.

Only God can reveal anything about Himself to His creation. He revealed enough of Himself in the scriptures to create hunger and desire inside our hearts, so that we will seek Him further. This is where the Holy Spirit is crucial in the romantic alluring of the created human heart. A person can read God's Word a thousand times with the comprehension of the physical human spirit and obtain lots of information about God. A different person can read the same Bible just one time under the influence of the Holy Spirit and come to the intimate knowledge of God. It takes God to reveal God, and without Him doing the revealing your spirit will obtain facts about God but not come to the knowing of God. The Holy Spirit's main goal is to cause you to fall madly in love with Jesus. This alluring from God's Spirit occurs as a person seeks more of Him. This usually takes place during Bible study, worship, or prayer. Too many Christians enter into these with repetitive, incognizant, physical attempts to encounter God and little expectation or preparation for the event. When you attempt to bring super reality into normal reality you need to be prepared! In focused prayer or energetic praise or devoted study, be prepared to enter a brilliance that bruises, that hurts, that tears the human spirit away from the control of the flesh.

Once you enter into the throne room light by the power of the Holy Sprit and then come back, everything else is dark. This world is dark compared to the light of God's throne room, and it is this Light that helps us deal with this dark world. He allures you with His light. Once the light of God illuminates a human heart, there is an occurrence that captivates it and causes an overflow of delirium and ecstasy that creates passionate hunger for more of God.

Hosea is a book in the Bible that reveals the Allure of God and the response of man with his intense yearning for the truest form of intimacy, love, and pleasure. You will read how a faithful God moves in the midst of His bride's adultery to allure her back into His embrace. God's Spirit will reveal in this book how He studies and moves to the fluctuating human heart, piercing when it needs to be pricked, embracing it at crucial moments of despair. He knows when to speak as a correcting leader and when to talk with gentle kindness as an alluring Lover. His unequivocal discernment allows Him to flow in and out of judgment and mercy incoherent to Satan and his followers. This allows us to respond to God's allure completely privileged to His account, therefore, not allowing any other force in the universe to be credited for winning humanity's heart. This attribute of God is why Satan was unable to discern that the murder of His Son was a victory not a defeat. The excruciating cry from Jesus on the cross held the weight of God's judgment of sin and at the same time released His extraordinary act of mercy. In your life there will be times when you feel as if God is judging and punishing you for your mistakes when He is actually unveiling His tender mercy and gentle allure to guide you to His river where He can bring you to the passion of energetic, youthful romantic love for Him. Look at what God tells His prophet Jeremiah to tell all of Israel:

> *"I remember you and the devotion of your youth, when you chased after Me in the wilderness. Israel was holy to me then".*
>
> *Jeremiah 2:2*

This is the purpose of the allure of God. No matter where you are in your sin or how deeply involved with your idolatrous lovers, God intensely desires to allure you away from where you are, and bring you to the place where His heart is intertwined to yours. Weather you have once chased after God passionately and now have become complacent, or if you have never began the chase, He yearns to create a passionate, youthful and vibrant love that burns within your heart for Him. Are you hungry for God? If so, locate the place where your hunger began, and you will find the beginning of the allure of God for your life. The beginning of God's alluring for you could also be called your Bethel. Let's look at God's allure in Jacobs's life.

"Returning To Your Bethel"

> *Then Jacob awoke from his sleep and said, "Surely the Lord is in this place, and I did not know it." He was afraid and said, "How awesome is this place! This is none other than the house of God, and this is the gate of heaven." So Jacob arose early in the morning and took the stone that he had put under his head and set it up as a pillar and poured oil on its top. He called the name of that place Bethel.*
>
> *Genesis 29:16-19*

> *Then God said to Jacob, "Arise up to Bethel and live there to God, Who appeared to you when you fled from your brother Esau. So Jacob said to His household and to all who were with him, "Put away the foreign gods which are among you, and purify yourselves and change your garments, and let us arise and go up to Bethel".*
>
> Genesis 35: 1-3

These significant passages are spiritual blueprints that reveal a window of divine intimacy and allure ordained by God. The Lord reveals His allure by inviting Jacob back to the place of intimacy, back to Bethel. Bethel is the place of romantic anointing where God set the intensity of the encounter and planted His seed of love in Jacob's heart. It is here that he became addicted to the overwhelming pleasure of God's presence. Bethel is where Jacob discovered the Anointed Rock Who symbolically is Christ Jesus and discover the gateway into eternal intimacy with Him.

As you read in Genesis, Jacob in the midst of his journey finds a rock to rest his weary head upon, and then God takes over from there. The sleeping head upon the Rock represents the surrendering of our authority over our lives to Christ's authority and headship. Jacob was tired of running, and God knew the perfect time to reveal Bethel to him. As I have already said, God works with the human heart in precise timing to create openness to Him. During Jacob's sleep, he dreams of a way to reach heaven. God reveals to Jacob that there is a way to come to Him and that He desires Jacob to come. If God did not want him to come, why would He reveal that there is a way? This dream reveals God's desire to allure people to Him. This revelation of God's heart always seems to stir the human heart by softening and preparing it for divine romance.

Jacob awakes from his sleep exhilarated by the encounter and driven by the passion of his heart as he declares; "Surely the Lord is in this place," and "How awesome is this place!" Encounters with the only true God are so overwhelming to the human spirit they are unforgettable to the human heart and mind. Usually a place or time is set as pillars to mark the encounter so that the person has a way of return. In this case and like many others throughout the Bible, God sets the time being morning and marks the place with the eternal symbol of everlasting life. Jacob arose early in the morning, I believe, filled with the Holy Spirit and prophetically takes his stone pillow and anoints it with oil setting it up as an eternal pillar symbolizing Christ the Anointed Stone.

The morning Jesus encountered me early and spoke to me similar words that I will never forget forever changed me. He said, "Awake every morning at this time, and I'll be here waiting for you." This was the place I knew I could always return to no matter how far away I might drift. For years I have strived to wake every morning at 5 to spend time with Jesus. It is the place where I have received most revelation from God and where I have felt His presence more frequently than anywhere else. My morning love walk through God's garden of intimacy is my Bethel! This is my house of God. It is where I am most at peace no matter what storm is stirring in my life. I long to awake to the dawn of God's glory, to smell the aroma of His sweetness, and join the morning critters in the serenity of their sounds. This place and time shines as a bright beacon of invitation to return to intimacy with God, no matter how dark my world is. This is what the Lord told Jacob in chapter 35 to return to his Bethel and this time to bring his family and leave all their idolatry behind. At Bethel God wants nothing to hinder Him from alluring you back to the place of intimacy.

"The Ability To Enjoy God"

"Oh how I love Your law! It is my meditation all the day"

Psalms 119:97

"Delight yourself in the Lord; And He will give you the desires of your heart"

Psalm 37:4

> *"The almighty will be your gold and choice silver to you.*
> *For then you will delight in the Almighty and lift up your*
> *face to God."*
>
> *Job 22:25-26*

The allure of God is driven by romantic emotions, and to be romanced is to be entertained. The feelings and emotions involved in romance entertain lovers. These emotions are some of the most powerful and exciting forms of entertainment known to man, and of course, our creator designed it this way. Jesus created these to create life and liveliness, not only to draw a man and woman together to make a baby, but also to create an alluring and exiting presence that draws man to God. Jesus has created a Divine entertainment hidden within the revelation and impartation of His beauty. He reveals His beauty and imparts it into our lives so we have the ability to enjoy the Fathers presence. As I said earlier, the Father dresses us in the Messiah's beauty so that, as His priest did in the former tabernacle we may also enter into His inner chamber to encounter Him. This level of entertainment supersedes all others and is absolutely priceless. It will over exhilarate your heart with a euphoria that will impact your world. The end time church will be surrounded by a society that is possessed by worldly entertainment, false pleasures, and demonic joys, which will occupy the day. This is why the end time church must find her highest entertainment from things of Divine power and supernatural delights. We must not allow ourselves to follow the pattern the world sets for society that is acceptable to unbelievers and is at our cost of fellowship with the Lord.

> *You are our letter, written in our hearts, known and read*
> *by all men; being manifested that you are a letter of Christ,*
> *cared for by us written not with ink but with the Spirit of*
> *the Living God, not on tablets of stone, but on tablets of*
> *human hearts.*
>
> *2 Corinthians 3:2&3*

The Lord does not desire to write a law letter for you again but rather a love letter to you with Christ's blood as the ink and the Holy Spirit as the pen, so that we would fall in love with Him. As He cried out in Hosea, *"You shall no longer call me master, but now you shall call Me Husband!"* Servants obey their masters out of fear and obligation, but a wife obeys her husband out of intimate love and adoration and this is the passion God is creating in His end time bride so that she finds her total enjoyment in Him and He can allure her away from all worldly entertainment.

Growing up I had a grandmother who took great pleasure and entertainment in serving and caring for her family. In all the years I have known her and the tens of thousands of meals I ate at her home, I have never once seen her sit down at the dinner table and eat a meal with her family. No matter what the occasion, whether a holiday or simply a Sunday afternoon get together, Grandma would not rest until everyone was satisfied, and then she would serve the coffee and dessert. I remember one time asking her why she did not just sit down with us and enjoy a relaxing meal and let me serve. She told me that I did not understand that serving her family and friends was one of her life's greatest forms of entertainment. Nothing pleased her more than to see everyone together, happy, and full. I believe God put that in my Grandma, because that's how He is. He desires to bring His church together and fill them with His unspeakable joy and pleasure. This personality of God is a good example of the contrast between worldly entertainment and divine entertainment.

God's desire in redemption is not to instruct us as to reveal our sins, so that we are guilt-ridden slaves to sin. He desires to impact our hearts with an overwhelming revelation of the immense affection and love He has for us. He creates hunger in our hearts for him by entertaining our senses and minds with His presence and beauty. The Holy Spirit romances us to the place of acceptance where the blood of Jesus becomes the permanent stain on our souls that turns the stone tablature of law into the broken vessel of a beautiful heart.

> *If the ministry of death in letters engraved on stones, came with glory, so that the sons of Israel could not look intently at the face of Moses because of the glory of his face, fading as it was, how will the ministry of the Spirit fail to be even more with glory? For if the ministry of condemnation has*

> *glory, much more does the ministry of righteousness abound
> in glory.*
>
> *2 Corinthians 3:7-9*

If Moses through the law had the shakana glory of intimacy with God, how much more should we under grace be experiencing the glory of intimacy with God in our lives? The glory of being intimately connected to God will awaken your heart to new levels of euphoria unreachable by human entertainment. Your hunger for this closeness is what you need to use to empower yourself to fast, obey, and to draw close to the glory mountain when everyone else fears it and stays away. In Exodus when God's glory rested upon the mountain, all the children of Israel stayed away gripped with fear, but Moses, with an intense desire to know God more, drew closer and closer to the mountain until he was surrounded by God's glory.

Experiencing this Divine entertainment and God's romantic allure requires obsession. You have to become so obsessed with your desire for Him that you are willing to do what is necessary to draw near. While everyone else stood back Moses drew near the dark thundering cloud where God was. Everyone around you might be what is holding you back from going up the mountain. Jesus responds to spiritual lovesickness. He comes to the one who is longing for Him and will not be content until He is found. A good example of this passion is found in the romantic chase described in Song of Solomon between the shulammite and the Beloved. This book becomes our fascinated reality as we pursue intimacy with the Lord. It holds deep revelation about our relationship with our Bridegroom God, and you will find great entertainment and delight as you begin to literally experience the divine romance described in the Song of Solomon and also other prophetic books of the Bible. This needs to become the end time church's occupation, entertainment, and passion, so that we do not fall into the devil's snares or deceptions that the world so passionately longs for. Let your chase for God's presence become the fulfillment of your days. Abandon your selfish impulses and replace these with devotion to the Word of God. Allow God's Spirit to set your spirit and your mind free from the distractions of life and begin to search deep into the heart of the intimate Father.

Divine entertainment is greatly about being fascinated with God by getting on the path of continual revelation. When God begins to reveal things to you that no man can intellectually speak on or figure out, you will start to become fascinated. He opens up windows of revealing about Himself, the Trinity, the world and even things about the enemy. He begins to release His presence into your realm and allows you to bask in it bringing a glorious glow to your perception. It is what Moses experienced on the mount when super reality became cognizant to normal reality.

There is something very important to understand about Divine entertainment and supernatural experiences that cannot be left out. God does not bring you to this point in your relationship with Him so you can go and become a famous preacher, a respected prophet, or to fulfill any selfish fantasies or desires you may have inside your heart. This is no televised miracle show open to public entertainment. It is an intimate, private, on-going relationship that has matured past the religious spirit, past the insecurity of rejection, and past the addictions of the flesh. A person who has been romanced by the Lord to the point of obsession most likely will become unpopular to Christians who choose to remain distant from God. Divine entertainment will not become a booster for your social status, but will boost your spiritual one to new levels, if you hold your experiences with God sacred and Holy.

There is nothing more degrading to a husband than when His wife shares there private intimacy to her friends and family, and the man always feels naked and exposed around these people. Some things need to always remain sacred and private in order to protect its blessing. Don't be so careless with the deep things God reveals to you that you cheapen it or rob God of His glory with selfish boasting. There are times God reveals things to a person that is to be shared with others for edification, warning, or inspiration but be assured that no man will receive the glory because of it. God creates hunger in our hearts for him by entertaining our senses and minds with His presence and beauty, for His enjoyment.

"Empowered By Joy"

Though the fig tree should not blossom and there be no fruit on the vines. Though the yield of the olive should fail and the fields produce no food. Though the flock should be cut off from the fold and there be no cattle in the stalls, Yet I will rejoice in the Lord, I will joy in the God of my salvation. The Lord God is my strength, and He has made my feet like hinds feet and makes me walk on my high places.

Habakkuk 3:17-19

If I should say, "My foot has slipped," Your loving kindness, O Lord, will hold me up. When my anxious thoughts multiply within me, Your consolations delight my soul.

Psalm 94: 18&19

Your life's delights will be your strength in times of trouble, and the power these delights carry will enable you to walk through. What do you delight yourself in? Where do you discover the most joy? What occupies the majority of your existence? These questions will reveal the source of your spiritual, mental, and sometimes physical stability that carries you through life.

The two scriptures above reveal the deep joy these writers carried that surpassed human intellect and dove into a super reality that only those who have an intimate fellowship with God can share in. The prophet Habakkuk comes to a place in his intimacy with God that enables him to see past the human needs and embrace the true thirst of humanity's soul, the pleasure of God's presence. As the psalmist also declares in the above scripture that when the finite or human power fails, such as the foot that slips or the anxious mind that torments, the eternal power of enjoyment in the Father's presence, strengthens the weary believer.

The joy of God's eternal presence will be the superior power in your life that will enable you to fulfill all His purposes. This ability to enjoy God will empower you and equip you above and beyond all human agencies. When man's sermons don't inspire you enough, His presence will. When false pleasures and temporary man made joys run dry, His presence will fill your cup to immeasurable limits. As I have said before, you have to desire God and become aware of His desire for you. The presence of Almighty God is as available as your availability to spend quiet time with Him. He responds to lovesickness and the passionate chase for His closeness. If your life is spent chasing popularity, wealth, comfort, repetition, or false pleasures, God will not come, because He will not be second. He must be first! He is a jealous God, and He wants to be your all, your first desire of the day, your hunger. He wants to be your fantasies come true. He longs to be in your thoughts and dreams. He desires to become the choice pleasure for your day and awaits the first word of the morning that is directed to Him from your heart. He delights in the one who makes Him their Lover above all else! His heart is stirred when a human soul takes Him with them everywhere they go and puts Him in the decision of everything they do. Walk with Him in the park in the cool of the day, enjoy romantic lovely worship on your bed at night, experience euphoric laughs as He reveals His humor to you in the noontime, and sit in the quiet of your prayer closet soaking in the immense love and desire of the Son as you study Him. His presence is a wonderland of joy and peace obtainable from any corner, alley, closet, or place on this earth. If you experience God's manifest closeness in your life, you will be empowered to overcome all obstacles, all addictions, all sins, every demon that spies on you, the deepest valley you face, and the highest mountain in your way, for nothing can weaken the one who dwells in the immense affection and beautiful embrace of the Lovely Lord of glory!

Chapter Five

THE YEARNING

"Desiring Fellowship"

Morning Love Affair

Draw me after you, my lovely King,
bring me into your inner chambers.
Release forth the fragrance of Your
desire for me. This divine arousal
of climbing upon Thine mountains,
leaping upon Thine hills. I search for
Thee whom my soul loves. Awaiting
the serenity of the dawn. Stirring on my bed
of anticipation, I yearn for our morning
love affair, were all is still, all
is sacred, all is seduced by Your
divine romance.

Considering the awesome otherness of the God who created everything, it overwhelms me that this same One would yearn for me. The day I recognized this reality my life and my heart changed forever. Most Christian religions teach facts, principals, laws, and inspiring stories about God and His holy Word but few really dig deep and comprehend the message of God's love for mankind. Understanding the way God reveals Himself to His creation is extremely essential for growth and maturity in life's most important relationship. Going deep into revelations of God requires a spiritual hunger and a yearning heart. After you have reached this point, God begins to unveil your spiritual eyes so you can look into personal thoughts and feelings that constantly dwell inside of Him, such as, His passionate desire to have intimate fellowship with you. There is not a second that passes in eternity that God is not longing for you. His variety of emotions such as His jealousy, His deep inner yearning, His euphoric thrills all well inside this beautiful heart and constantly are awakened and stirred at all His eye sees. When a person is awakened in holy romantic pleasure and falls in love with Jesus, God's Spirit and heart experiences unspeakable pleasure and joy that stirs the passion of all of heaven as billions of angels cry out in extravagant celebration and worship of the Lamb of God. When one of His believers is drawn away by other lovers and begins to chase them instead of Him, fiery jealousy ignites His divine action plan to win them back and destroy their false lovers. This is all going on continually inside God's holy habitation as He watches trillions of souls every second of every day.

"The Betrothal"

"I will betroth you to Me forever; Yes, I will betroth you to Me in righteousness and in justice, In loving-kindness and in compassion, And I will betroth you to Me in faithfulness. Then you will know the Lord".

Hosea 2: 19 & 20

This passage in Hosea reveals the literal marriage betrothal of God to you and the explanation of how He fulfills this miracle. According to the old law when a man desires the betrothal of a woman, he would have to pay a bride price to her father. If the father accepted then the two would marry. God's bride price consists of the many gifts of His divine lovely nature and attributes. These gifts hold the power and security that transforms the perishing into the eternal, defeats the powers and principalities of evil, and totally transform your life. God lavishes these blessings upon His bride as a husband covers her with his last name, proclaiming to all His everlasting love to her. He invigorates the church with His gentle touch and soothing voice reminding her throughout history of these blessings so that she overcomes.

God's desire for continued fellowship with mankind is why He betrothed Himself to us. He knew that the existence of evil and pride would attack at the very heart of the human and divine connection attempting to stop it in every aspect. The betrothal of God is an essential revelation to every believer searching for the way into consistent fellowship with their God and experiencing every obstacle created to stop them.

"Betrothed in Righteousness"

I will rejoice greatly in the Lord, My soul will exalt in my God; For He has clothed me with garments of salvation, He has wrapped me with a robe of righteousness, as a bridegroom decks himself with a garland, And as a bride adorns herself with her jewels.

Isaiah 61: 10

God eternally sealed His bride by wrapping her in His Son's righteousness in which He offers us the promise of sanctification and justification. Those who receive the miracle of God's grace, His eternal life through Christ, will be clothed with wedding garments of salvation and then wrapped in beautiful robes of divine righteousness. The first bride price God offers is to dress us in acceptable clothing of divine extravagant beauty. As we learned already this eternal righteousness leads to the sanctification and justification of God's church so that we may continually enter into intimate fellowship with the Creator. He wraps us in His Son's righteousness to allow the fullest deepest intimate embrace the Father can bestow on us. Our fallen nature would impede the embrace of God due to His holiness. Therefore, by covering our sins in Christ righteousness, God is able to fully embrace His perfect, sinless Son. This is why Isaiah tells us to greatly rejoice for God has allowed fallen humanity to still experience the highest pleasure, the utmost joy, in the arms of almighty God. Those who come to the saving grace of God through the Messiah Christ Jesus will experience God's holy romantic passionate embrace as He betroths you to His Son, in righteousness.

The Lord is my Shepherd, I shall not want. He makes me lie down in green pastures; He leads me besides quite waters. He restores my soul; He guides me is paths of righteousness for His name's sake.

Psalm 23

The righteousness of Jesus Christ carries eternal benefits as well as mortal ones. In the passage above the Lord reveals a promise to guide us in paths of righteousness for His name's sake. This righteousness of Christ cannot be put to shame by anyone as to say; "it was not adequate for lives journey". The righteousness we receive eternally holds a proud, majestic, and glorious quality to it. We are sealed and made presentable to the Father through this gift from Jesus. It is precious, priceless, and absolutely the greatest treasure discovered by any human ever. Nothing can be held in higher value then the free gift of eternal righteousness in Christ Jesus. This is its eternal appearance. The mortal identity of this freely bestowed righteousness differs from its eternal brother. Although its value is equal, the rewards are opposite. The paths of this life are anything but glorious and paved with gold. That's what is awaiting those who make it across the finish line. Do not be convinced by the prosperity, comfort first, preachers of our days who says that our life journey will be chocolate cake if you have enough faith in God, because finishing this race of life well does not change based on a persons bank account. This life's race is not a pretty one and don't think your going to be the one who slips through the battles untouched. The prize is not to be rewarded before the race is finished. Have you ever witnessed a race where the first prize was given to a person who never crossed the finish line? Remember, the pleasures of this life are ephemeral. They don't sustain a human but for the moment. This is the main reason why the trends of our society constantly change and everyone is longing for the next great thing to fulfill their lives. This is where mortal righteousness enters in. By guiding us on paths of righteousness God invigorates the human heart with eternal divine pleasures, or superior pleasures that enables us to finish the race, to stay the course, and to be over-comers to all battles we will face. This is the confusion of prosperity preachers. They have such a strong emphasis on mortal rewards and pleasures causing a person to attempt drawing near to God with motives that will only hinder the much-desired intimacy God has for us. God will not allow you to experience the pleasures of His presence if you are telling Him you love Him and are worshiping Him so that you will receive mortal blessings. Who is actually saying to God that they desire Him so they can get a new car, or land the perfect job they want? To your surprise I would venture to say that it's the majority of religion. Ask yourself this, what does your prayers and the prayers of others mostly consist of Request or adoration? Are you always going to God with your needs or do you ever speak to God with pure heartfelt affection or words of appreciation for Who He is and not just what He has done for you?

The righteousness we experience on this earth will consistently lead us besides the still waters of divine pleasures. When everything is in an uproar, it will cause us to lie still in green pastures of revealed heavenly beauty. Christ righteousness will prepare a table before the worst enemy of our days causing us to remain in His presence, keeping our focus on the eternal reward, not valuing this life's pleasures over Him. The mortal righteousness Christ dresses us in gives us His ability to walk on this earth as He did, remaining heavenly in our minds, in our actions, and in our focus. The Apostle Paul wrote that He is constantly forgetting what was in the past and pressing forth to the eternal goals and rewards. His focus was on the eternal values not on this world's because he was given the mind of Christ, the righteousness that is given to believers while on this earth.

God absolutely knew what it would take to bring man back into the unbridled intimacy He first created in the Garden of Eden. This is what He yearns for; it is the desired fellowship, the beauty of our free will love for Him, when we affectionately worship Him with hearts of perfected praise, when God romantically walked with Adam in the cool of the day. He betrothed us in righteousness to fulfill the yearning of His lovely heart to embrace us in all aspects of our existence, now and forever as we come to the marriage supper of the Lamb.

"Betrothed in Justice"

Then I saw a great white throne and Him who sat upon it, from whose presence earth and heaven fled away, and no place was found for them. And I saw the dead, the great and the small, standing before the throne, and books were open; and another book was opened, which is the book of life; and the dead were judged from the things which were written in the books according to their deeds.

Revelation 20: 11&12

If another human decided our eternal judgement we absolutely all would burn in hell. How I can say this is, if anyone of us saw what only the Almighty God could see, we would hate the world! In our day and age people can't let go of the petty and little sins that occur between friends and family and even church family. We get angry over someone cutting us off on the highway or a person who jumps in front of you in a crowded line. We loose our love and peace over the smallest, insignificant stuff that occurs everyday. How could anyone possibly love the world like God does if we could see every sinful thought, if we heard every ugly word spoken, if we felt the pain of every victim of crime? What if every time a baby was brutally murdered you witnessed it first hand and felt the pain as if it was your own child! Or every girl that was raped you had to experience her inner torment, her physical and emotional decay. Immagine feeling the painful hours of tears that slowly creates a hardened shell around her once soft and gentle heart. Then you had to look at the face of her attacker and love him knowing what he just did to your very own child. Imagine looking at this man that just destroyed your daughter's life and still love him enough to desire eternal life for him. WHO CAN DO THIS BUT GOD HIMSELF! We have a hard enough time watching the evening news and simply hearing about things that goes on without becoming paranoid, bitter people. Again, if we had to see and feel what God does we would hate the world. Therefore, what is true justice? The perfect God who had no sin subjected Himself to the hands of men who sinned thousands of times and allowed them to brutally murder Him. Is that justice? The justice of God is so majestic and so very honorable that it should be held most precious to our hearts. God lavishes upon His church a justice that is incomparable to any other form of justice that exists. He eternally justifies anyone who response to His love with an open heart. The Lord yearns to justify humanity and once again have the intimate and uninhibited fellowship He once had with us in the Garden of Eden. This is what the marriage supper of the Lamb is about. When the justice of God is completed and His bride has been made ready, He is going to prepare a feast to celebrate the greatest moment of eternity. For then the yearning of God's lovely heart will be fulfilled.

"Betrothed in Loving-kindness"

By loving-kindness and truth iniquity is atoned for, And by the fear of the Lord one keeps away from evil.

Proverbs 16: 6

But You, O Lord, are a God merciful and gracious, Slow to anger and abundant in loving-kindness and truth.

Psalm 86: 15

The fear mentioned in the above verses is defined as reverence, respect, honor, and humility. The loving-kindness of God brings a person to the fear of God. The more God demonstrates His unconditional love in your life the more reverence you will have for Him. There is an increase of the intensity in passion that comes forth from a person when they come to this point in thier betrothal with the Lord. We learned what the righteousness and justice of God does for a person who falls in love with Him. Now we will see how His loving-kindness literally ignites a flame of passion inside your heart.

As I said earlier, God studies the fluctuations of the human heart and deciphers the openness a person has to receive deeper levels of revelation about Himself, His heart, and His love. The more openness your heart has toward eternal realms and understandings about divine love and divine purposes, the more God will reveal things to you. This openness does not seem to come as a result of anything man can do but seems to only occur as a response to God's loving-kindness or Grace. Grace is a New Testament word for the Old Testament definition of God's loving-kindness. Grace is defined as unmerited favor. Therefore God demonstrates this undeserved favor in revelations of His loving-kindness and tender mercies. The more you experience God's loving-kindness, the more open your heart and spirit will become to receiving deeper eternal things, things about the heart of God and the personality of each Person of the Trinity, the passion that stirs between these three personalities in the Godhead. There are many fascinating revelations about our existence that God longs to reveal to each of us. That is why we where created and why God made this universe. We were made for His pleasure and this universe was given for our pleasure. Had we not sinned in Eden, we would have always had pleasurable experiences in our lives and we would not have any pain and suffering. Even though we blew it, God in His loving-kindness still made a way for us to experience the loveliness and beauty of His creation when He redeemed mankind with His Son's sacrifice. This sacrifice is another revelation of an extraordinary act of God's loving-kindness and tender mercy. The greatest moment in all of history was the Crucifixion of Jesus. According to the Gospels account of this, right after Jesus breathed His last breath, the veil of the temple was torn in half. As we discovered earlier, this veil was the entrance of God's most sacred, holy place called the holy of holies were He would reveal His manifest presence. Out of all the things God could have done at this most crucial event in time, He opens His inner chambers, so that all men can enter into intimacy with Him. After He paid the ultimate price, God steps to the podium of the world and opens His beautiful heart to all and asked everyone to look at His innermost passion, His strongest desire, His unconditional love, and see that He actually desires you this much. God exposed Himself with a sort of divine humility, revealing that there is no length He is unwilling to go to restore close fellowship with humanity. This is the passion of the cry from the cross as Jesus screams in agony; "My God, my God, why have You forsaken me!" At this moment in time the heart of God was exposed in a mysteriously beautiful scene of divine love. I almost wish I could hear the Fathers response to His Son's cry as the heavens shake from the thundering scream coming out of the very throne in heaven responding; "Because I love them so much, with all my heart, with my entire mind with all I Am! This is why I did this Son, because I can't live without them!!!" The loving-kindness of the yearning God revealed by a moment of passion, jealousy, and fiery love is the greatest known act of humility known to man. This is a God who logs for His bride and awaits the moments in eternity that expose His hearts true desire, His true inner yearning, His betrothal in loving-kindness.

"Releasing a Heavenly Fragrance"

While Jesus was in Bethany at the home of Simon the leper, and reclining at the table, there came a woman with an alabaster vial of very costly perfume of pure nard; and she broke the vial and poured it over His head. But some were indignant remarking to one another, why has this perfume been wasted? For this perfume might have been sold for over three hundred denarii's, and the money given to the poor, and they were scolding her. But Jesus said, "Let her alone; why do you bother her? She has done a good deed to Me. For you always have the poor with you, and whenever you wish you can do good to them, but you do not always have Me. She has done what she could; she has anointed My body before hand for burial. Truly I say to you, whenever the gospel is preached in the whole world, what this woman has done will also be spoken of in memory of her.

The Gospel of Mark 14: 3-9

There is a beautiful fragrance released from those who are in love with God. As the lovesick woman who broke her alabaster jar, poring out her deepest, most passionate worship upon her Lord, we too can release a pleasing aroma of intimate worship when we give Jesus our real "in love" passionate affection. It's the fragrance of true love, of devotion, coming from the heart of a soul who has fallen madly in love with Jesus! Such a heavenly aroma is so uncommon to the ordinary church attendee that it often escapes their limited awareness, seeping through the isles of the church mysteriously unnoticed. Just like the religious leaders who sat at the table eating and drinking there preplanned pleasures with Jesus, they were completely unaware of the deep yearning inside the Lords heart who was invited to dine with them. This yearning was for more than dinner and fellowship, more then preplanned service and the carefully selected order in which this time was set aside. This hunger dwelling so deep inside the Lord's heart was a hunger for a more intimate, more passionate type of fellowship. But the religious was unaware, too caught up in their traditional chat as the smell of their orthodox aroma filled this typical gathering place for them. However, as divine fate, or shall I say divine romance, would have it, the Lord's yearning would be fulfilled. Suddenly, the men in the room are alarmed as a woman rushes in the door. Though uninvited and unwanted she makes her way to the feet of Jesus with such a passion in her eyes that nothing could break her focus. Then in an act of unbridled, romantic passion, she lavishes upon her Lord a worship that satiates His heart like a rush of spring water upon a sun-scorched head. As streams of tears flow from her eyes, she breaks open the veil releasing a fragrance so heavenly that the entire room is filled with wonderment. The look on Jesus' face, the tears in His holy eyes reveal a moment of eternal satisfaction, almost like a dry rose revitalized by a noon rain. Such a lovely moment of beauty and romance shared between two hearts connecting with each other. This was no preplanned worship event but rather the overflow of passion from a person who recognizes the loveliness and beauty of God. I remember an old man name Ralph who I had the privilege of ministering to for the last two years of his life before I closed the final chapter message for his loved ones at his funeral. Most people who attended church with old man Ralph did not even notice something he did every Sunday morning. I'm sure they saw him do this many times but I don't think they really knew the true essence of what old man Ralph was doing. I did not fully become aware of this acts true meaning until I began spending more one on one time with him and then God opened my eyes to see the beauty of such an aromatic heart. Every Sunday morning old man Ralph would wake early with the singing birds and go out to his garden in his back yard where he would quietly, and romantically talk to Jesus. Before heading of to church old man Ralph would pick a handful of the most blossomed lilies in his garden. When he showed up at church always a few minutes early, this old hunched back man who could barley walk a straight line, would mysteriously make his way through the isles of the church undisturbed by greetings, almost unnoticed by the rest though leaving a heavenly fragrance of freshly plucked lilies as he passed you. See you couldn't be talking or focusing on the typical Sunday morning sanctuary chatter. In order to truly see what was happening you had to be in worship. Your focus had to be that of the passionate woman who disrupted the ordinary in order to lavish an extraordinary love upon a worthy focus. As old man Ralph reached the altar area he would carefully, but romantically place the bouquet of lilies upon the altar, then kneel in worship at the feet of his true love. Isn't that what we do to the ones we are truly in love with? Don't we bring them flowers? It took me a long time to become aware of the heavenly fragrance old man Ralph released from his heart every day but when I did, everything in my life changed. Are you releasing a heavenly fragrance of an intimate relationship with God from your in love heart? I believe old man Ralph is, still to this day up in heaven at the eternal altar of God. At times I dream of this, and see him tending a beautiful garden in paradise which produces eternal lilies more breathtaking then we can imagine. And Ralph bringing them to His eternal Lover's feet and fulfilling the yearning inside the lovely heart of Jesus. Will you be?

In closing, let's look at the love language God uses to consummate eternity's goals. By now I hope that you have a desire to get to know God more, and to begin seeking His presence in your everyday life. If not, please reread this book slower and more thoroughly and ask the Holy Spirit to reveal Himself to you. If you now have an ember of fire burning inside your soul, and you are longing for intimate moments with God, then apply the principals you learned in this book and begin to create an atmosphere that God desires to come to on this earth. Remember, He is the one that was willing to lay down all His glory in heaven to become a human and go to the torture of the cross, so that you may have this intimacy with Him. Therefore it is your desire that has to line up with His, not His desire agreeing with yours. Allow the following scriptures and all God's Holy Word to romance you into His intimate bridal chambers in your world until He chooses to bring you to His in His world.

Let us make man in Our image according to Our likeness.

{Genesis 1:26}

Now the Lord appeared to Him by the oaks of Mamre; Abraham said: Please let a little water be brought and wash your feet, and rest yourselves under the tree.

{Genesis 18: 1 & 4 paraphrased}

In Your loving-kindness You have led the people whom You have redeemed; In Your strength You have guided them to Your Holy habitation.

{Exodus 15: 13}

Let them construct a sanctuary for Me, that I may dwell among them.

{Exodus 25: 8}

Thus you are to be holy to Me, for I the Lord is holy; and I have set you apart from the peoples to be Mine.

{Leviticus 20: 26}

I will make My dwelling among you, and My soul will not reject you. I will also walk among you and be your God, and you shall be My people.

{Leviticus 26: 11-12}

So the Lord said, "I have pardoned them according to your word; but indeed as I live, all the earth will be filled with the glory of the Lord".

{Numbers 14: 20 &21}

The oracle of Him who hears the words of God, And knows the knowledge of the Most High, who sees the vision of the Almighty, falling down, yet having eyes uncovered.

{Numbers 24: 16}

You came near and stood at the very foot of the mountain, and the mountain burned with fire to the very heart of the heavens;

{Deuteronomy 4: 11}

For the Lord your God is a consuming fire a jealous God.
{Deuteronomy 4: 24}

Consecrate yourselves, for tomorrow the Lord will do wonders among you.
{Joshua 3: 5}

Now therefore put away the foreign gods which are in your midst, and incline your hearts to the Lord the God of Israel.
{Joshua 24: 23}

Thus let all Your enemies perish O Lord; But let those who love Him be like the rising of the sun in its might.
{Judges 5: 31}

The sons of Israel inquired of the Lord (for the Ark of the covenant of God was there in those days).
{Judges 20: 27}

Wash yourself therefore, and anoint yourself and put on your best clothes, and go down to the threshing floor, but do not make yourself known to the man until he has finished eating and drinking.
{Ruth 3: 3}

zt happened in the middle of the night that the man was startled and bent forward and behold, a woman was lying at his feet. He said who are you? And she answered, I am Ruth your maid. So spread your covering over your maid, for you are a close relative.
{Ruth 3: 8&9}

But I will raise up for myself a faithful priest who will do according to what is in my heart and in my soul.

{1 Samuel 2: 35}

And the Lord appeared again at Shiloh because the Lord revealed Himself to Samuel at Shiloh by the Word of the Lord.

{1 Samuel 3: 21}

And David was dancing before the Lord with all his might, and David was wearing the linen ephod.

{2 Samuel 6: 14}

He also brought me forth into a broad place; He rescued me because He delighted in me.

{2 Samuel 22: 20}

I will dwell among the sons of Israel and will not forsake my people Israel.

{1 Kings 6: 13}

The Lord said to him, " I have heard your prayer and your supplication, which you have made before me; I have consecrated this house which you have built by putting My name there forever, and My eyes and My heart will be there perpetually".

{1 Kings 9: 3}

I have heard your prayer, I have seen your tears; behold I will heal you. On the third day you shall go up to the house of the Lord.

{2 Kings 20: 5b}

Because your heart was tender and you humbled yourself before the Lord.

{2 Kings 22: 19a}

So he left Asaph and his relatives there before the Ark of the covenant of the Lord to minister before the Ark continually as every day's work required.

{1 Chronicles 16: 37}

Serve Him with a whole heart and a willing mind for the Lord searches all hearts, and understands every intent of the thoughts. If you seek Him, He will let you find Him.

{1 Chronicles 28: 9b}

In unison when the trumpeters and the singers were to make themselves heard with one voice to praise and to glorify the Lord, and when they lifted up their voice accompanied by trumpets and cymbals and instruments of music, and when they praised the Lord saying, " He indeed is good for His loving kindness is everlasting, then the house, the house of the Lord, was filled with a cloud. So that the priest could not stand to minister because of the cloud, for the glory of the Lord filled the house of God.

{2 Chronicles 5: 13 & 14}

Those from all the tribes of Israel who set their hearts on seeking the Lord.... He did evil because he did not set his heart to seek the Lord.

{2 Chronicles 11: 16 & 12: 14}

the people could not distinguish the sound of the shout of joy from the sound of the weeping of the people....

{Ezra 3: 12a}

For Ezra had set his heart to study the law of the Lord and to practice it.

{Ezra 7: 10a}

For all the people were weeping when they heard the words of the Law.

{Nehemiah 8: 9b}

He read from the book of the law of God daily.

{Nehemiah 8: 18a}

He reveals mysteries from the darkness and brings the deep darkness into light.

{Job 12: 22}

The Almighty will be your gold and choice silver to you. For then you will delight in the Almighty, and lift up your face to God.

{Job 22: 25 & 26}

The Lord has looked down from heaven upon the sons of men to see if there are any who understand, who seek after God.

{Psalms 14: 2}

You make him joyful with gladness in Your presence.

{Psalm 21: 6b}

O Lord I love the habitation of Your house and the place where Your glory dwells.

{Psalm 26: 8}

One thing I ask that will I seek,that I may dwell in the house of the Lord all the days of my life, to behold the beauty of the Lord, and to meditate in His temple.

{*Psalm 27: 4*}

You hide them in the secret place of Your presence from the conspiracies of man.

{*Psalm 31: 20*}

They looked to Him and were radiant and their faces will never be ashamed.

{*Psalm 34: 5*}

They drink their fill of the abundance of Your house; And You give them drink from the river of Your pleasures.

{*Psalm 36: 8*}

For the devious are an abomination to the Lord; But He is intimate with the upright.

{*Proverbs 3: 32*}

Then I was besides Him, as a master workman; And I was daily His delight.

{*Proverbs 8: 30*}

He has set eternity in their hearts....

{*Ecclesiastes 3: 11*}

Guard your steps as you go to the house of God and draw near to listen rather than to offer the sacrifice of fools.

{*Ecclesiastes 5: 1*}

Draw me after You and let us run together! The King has brought me into His chambers.

{*Song of Songs 1: 4*}

He has brought me to His banquet hall, And His banner over me is love.

{*Song of Songs 2: 4*}

Your eyes will see the King in His beauty;

{*Isaiah 33: 17*}

I will give you the treasures of darkness and the hidden wealth of secret places so that you may know that it is I, The Lord, the God of Israel Who calls you by your name.

{*Isaiah 45: 3*}

I remember concerning you the devotion of your youth, the love of your betrothals, your following after Me in the wilderness.

{*Jeremiah 2: 2*}

But you are a harlot with many lovers; yet you turn to Me, declares the Lord.

{*Jeremiah 3: 1*}

I have called to my lovers, but they have deceived Me. My priest and My elders perished in the city while they sought food to restore their strength themselves.

{*Lamentations 1: 19*}

(In jealously), He has violently treated His tabernacle like a garden booth; He has destroyed His appointed meeting place.

{Lamentations 2: 6 parenthesis added}

How I have been hurt by their adulterous hearts which turned away from Me, and by their idols...

{Ezekiel 6: 9b}

Then I passed by you and saw you, and behold, You were at the time for love; so I spread My skirt over you and covered your nakedness. I Also swore to you and entered into a covenant with you so that you became Mine, declares the Lord.

{Ezekiel 16: 8}

....for from the first day that you set your heart on understanding this and on humbling yourself before your God, your words were heard, and I have come in response to your words.

{Daniel 10: 12}

Those who have insight will shine brightly like the brightness of the expanse of heaven.

{Daniel 12: 3a}

Therefore behold I will allure her, bring her into the wilderness and speak kindly to her.

{Hosea 2: 14}

I will betroth you to me forever, yes I will betroth you to me in righteousness and in justice, in loving kindness and in compassion.

{*Hosea 2: 19*}

Let the Bridegroom come out of His room and the Bride out of her bridal chamber.

{*Joel 2: 16b*}

Behold I am going to send you grain, new wine and oil, and you will be satisfied in full with them.

{*Joel 2: 19b*}

I will pass through the midst of you, says the Lord.

{*Amos 5: 17b*}

In that day I will raise up the tabernacle of David and wall up its breaches.....

{*Amos 9: 11*}

because He delights in unchanging love.

{*Micah 7: 18c*}

The Lord God is my strength, and He has made my feet like hind's feet and makes me walk on my high places.

{*Habakkuk 3: 17*}

Every morning He brings His justice to light, He does not fail.

{*Zephaniah 3: 5b*}

The Lord God is in your midst, A victorious warrior, He will exalt over you with joy, He will be quiet in His love, He will rejoice over you with shouts of joy.

{*Zephaniah 3: 17*}

I will make you a signet ring, for I have chosen you, declares the Lord of host.

{*Haggai: 2: 23c*}

I am exceedingly jealous for Jerusalem and Zion.

{*Zachariah 1: 14b*}

Be silent all flesh before the Lord for He is aroused from His holy habitation.

{*Zachariah 2: 13*}

But for you who fear my name, the Sun of righteousness will rise with healing in its wings; and you will go forth and skip about the calves from the stall.

{*Malachi 4: 2*}

But you when you pray, go into your inner room, close your door and pray to your Father who is in secret, and your Father Who sees what is done in secret will reward you.

{*Matthew 6: 6*}

The Bridegroom came and those who were ready went in with Him to the wedding feast and the door was shut.

{*Matthew 25: 10b*}

Early in the morning, while it was still dark Jesus got up, left the house, and went away to a secluded place, and was praying there.

{Mark 1: 35}

It was at this time that He went off to the mountain to pray, and He spent the whole night in prayer to God.

{Luke 6: 12}

Mary then took a pound of very costly perfume of pure nard, and anointed the feet of Jesus and wiped His feet with her hair.

{John 12: 3}

It was at this time that Moses was born; and he was lovely in the sight of God.

{Acts 7: 20b}

and He made from one man every nation of mankind to live on all the face of the earth, having determined their appointed times and the boundaries of their habitation. That they would seek God, if perhaps they might grope for Him and find Him, though He is not far from each one of us.

{Acts 17: 26 & 27}

But God demonstrates His own love for us, in that while we were yet sinners, Christ died for us.

{Romans 5: 8}

Do you know that you are a temple of God and that the Spirit of God dwells in you?

{1 Corinthians 3: 16}

But the one who joins himself to the lord is one spirit with Him.

{1 Corinthians 6: 17}

For I am jealous for you with a Godly jealousy; for I betrothed you to one Husband, so that to Christ I might present you as a pure virgin.

{2 Corinthians 11: 2}

But now you have come to know God, or rather to be known by God.....

{Galatians 4: 9a}

in whom you also are being built together into a dwelling of God in the Spirit

{Ephesians 2: 22}

Finally, brethren, whatever is true, whatever is honorable, whatever is right, whatever is pure, whatever is lovely, whatever is of good repute, if there is any excellence and if anything worthy of praise, dwell on these things. (Is not God all these things?)

{Philippians 4: 8 parenthesis added}

For it was the Fathers good pleasure for all the fullness to dwell in Him.

{Colossians 1: 19}

For you have died and your life is hidden with Christ in God.

{Colossians 3: 3}

whether we are awake or sleep, we will live together with Him.

{*1 Thessalonians 5: 10*}

May the Lord direct your hearts into the love of God and into the steadfastness of Christ.

{*2 Thessalonians 3: 5*}

Now she who is a widow indeed and who has been left alone, has fixed her hope on God and continues in entreaties and prayers night and day.

{*1 Timothy 5: 5*}

.....on God Who richly supplies you with all things to enjoy.

{*1 Timothy 6: 17c*}

and He is the radiance of His glory and the exact representation of His nature.

{*Hebrews 1: 3*}

Let us draw near with a sincere heart in full assurance of faith.....

{*Hebrews 10: 22a*}

Without faith it is impossible to please Him.(Or to say, to bring pleasure to God)

{*Hebrews 11: 6 parentheses added*}

Draw near to God and He will draw near to you.

{*James 4: 8*}

But you are a chosen race, a royal priesthood, A holy nation, a people for God's own possession...
{*1 Peter 2: 9a*}

For this is the love of God, that we keep His commandments and His commandments are not burdensome; (but rather pleasurable}
{*1 John 5: 3 parentheses added*}

Keeping yourselves in the love of God, waiting anxiously for the mercy of our Lord Jesus Christ to eternal life.
{*Jude 1: 21*}

But I have this against you, that you left your first love.
{*Revelation 2: 4*}

Let us rejoice and be glad and give glory to Him, for the marriage of the Lamb has come and His bride has made herself ready. Then he said to me, write Blessed are those who are invited to the marriage supper of the Lamb...
{*Revelation 19: 7 & 9*}

And I saw the holy city, new Jerusalem, coming down out of heaven from God, made ready as a bride adorned for her husband.
{*Revelation 21: 2*}

THE SPIRIT AND THE BRIDE SAY, " COME". AND LET THE ONE WHO HEARS SAY, "COME". AND LET THE ONE WHO IS THIRSTY COME; LET THE ONE WHO WISHES TAKE THE WATER OF LIFE WITHOUT COST.
{*REVELATION 22: 17*}

Morning love walk

My gracious love, Creator of light,
mirror Your passion within me.
I can see You this morning my love
as I gaze through the window.
I delight to see Your fellowship with
the chirpy morning singers. I jealously
desire their sacred moments with
You. I relate to these little worshipers,
as they do their enchanted dance around You.
I know their longing to find rest on Your arm,
If we could only rest our weary heads upon Your
chest, never to return to our carnal reality.
Only if we could hear You whisper
Your lovely songs in our hearts and hear your
divine romantic talk, we may never choose
to leave you Lord, but always remain in
Your gracious morning love walk.

Sweet Healing Psalm

Listen to the voice of your Lover
as He whispers sweet healing
in your hear. Arise your eyes to
Thine mountain for you know great
joy is near. Allow the freedom of
singing calm the rain, then hold fast
to the melody till He numbs the pain.
Hold fast dear saint, the supper is near,
keep writing your song with trembling
and fear. Till then shall we sing when
the time is told, and then shall we dance,
dear saint, on the streets that are gold.

I wait for You Lord,
Amongst still waters,
You have drawn me to this place.
As I lay in Your golden fields
I have drifted away into
the glory of Your creation,
although I lay still, I am still no more.
My ears are filled with melodic worship.
I applaud with you, sweet birch,
old maple, oh how worthy He is!
My eyes are filled with tears of joy;
I sing with you lovely wind,
the eternal hymns you and the soy
valley sings in polished harmony.
Father, I join in the groaning of the
deep. The waters who make
intercession for all it sees.
All creation longs for You Beloved.
Come lay still with us Lord,
arise in this morning's dew.
Whisper with me sweet Jesus,
I rejoice with all of nature,
for all creation delights in You.

The End,

but hopefully

a beginning for you.

Printed in the United States
116993LV00002B/225/A

9 781425 936556